The Warning of Kashmir

By

G.S. RAGHVAN

ANMOL PUBLICATIONS PVT LTD
New Delhi 110 002

ANMOL PUBLICATIONS PVT LTD
4374/4B, Ansari Road
Daryaganj, New Delhi-110 002

Reprint 1993
ISBN 81-7041-824-0

PRINTED IN INDIA
Published by J.L. Kumar for Anmol Publications Pvt Ltd, New Delhi
and Printed at Mehra Offset Press, Delhi.

PREFACE

WRITTEN with every variety of purpose, books on Kashmir are legion. Of absorbing interest to archæologist or historian, and lovelier far, as has been truthfully said, than an artist might imagine in his dreams, this wonder-spot of the world has been home alike to the recluse and the voluptuary. The great Kalhana placed learning first among the fragrant offerings of "the region which Kailasa lights up with his dazzling snow, and which the tossing Ganga clothes with a soft garment"; and an enraptured Moghul sovereign exclaimed,

> "If there be a Paradise on earth,
> It is here, it is here, it is here."

Unhappily, this small volume does not contain the outpourings of ecstasy. It has to do with sordid things; it is designed to call attention, in plain and prosaic language, to an exigent problem,—of moment to the people as well as the governments of the Indian States and British India. Kashmir has suggested the theme both because of the peculiar position of the State involving far-reaching questions and of the pernicious agitation recently directed against it. The narrative in this book and the warning uttered in it are the result of anxious study at first-hand of a distressing situation. There is no picturesque prevarication here, but only an unadorned statement of truth. Should this unsentimental recital of facts avail to restore a perspective which has been distorted in the recent agitation, the writer's purpose will have been adequately fulfilled.

The writer is immensely grateful to the numerous people in the State whose assistance has been invaluable to him in elucidating facts. He also desires to express his thanks to the authorities for loans of books from the Public Library.

SRINAGAR,
7th September, 1931. G. S. R.

CONTENTS

THE WARNING OF KASHMIR.

I

ADVENT OF DOGRA RAJPUTS

THE settled and reposeful existence of the inhabitants of Kashmir practically begins with the advent of the Dogra Rajput rule in the middle of the nineteenth century. Before that period, save for a few welcome, and occasionally considerably long, breaks, life to them was one unrelieved state of turmoil and tribulation. The territories now known as Jammu and Kashmir State comprise Jammu, Ladakh, Baltistan, Kashmir and Gilgit. As described by official records, "they occupy a unique position in the geography of the Indian Empire. Situated in the north-western extremity of India, the Jammu and Kashmir State has a boundary line of several hundred miles touching Tibet, Chinese Turkistan and Russian Turkistan. The three empires of Britain, China and Russia meet on its frontier. The area of Jammu and Kashmir is 84,258 square miles. The country is almost entirely mountainous varying in height from hillocks on the

Punjab border to the great Himalayan and Karakoram ranges. Among these are ensconced many valleys, of which Kashmir is the best known. The valley of Kashmir is more or less a level plain, 1,600 square miles in area, surrounded on all sides by mountains which has made access to it very difficult. The mountains may conveniently be classified into three divisions: (1) The region of the Outer Hills, comprising the long ranges to the immediate north of the Punjab and rising to an altitude of 2,000 to 4,000 feet above the sea level. This is mostly bare or covered with scrub; (2) the region of the Middle Mountains ranging on the average between 8,000 and 10,000 feet in height, though many of the peaks are 14,000 to 15,000 feet high. The valley of Kashmir forms part of this region; (3) beyond this great range, the whole tract (except Gilgit and the adjacent territories on the north and north-west) is at a high level and in a geographical sense, may be said to belong to Tibet. The ranges here vary from 17,000 to more than 22,000 feet in height, and one peak has an altitude of 28,265 feet and is the second highest known peak in the world." According to the census of 1931, the total population of the State is 36,45,339, of which 17,88,393 inhabit the province of Jammu; 15,69,394 represent the population of the Kashmir Province, while the rest belong to the Frontier tracts which have an area of 63,560 square miles.

Before Maharaja Gulab Singh consolidated these territories under his rule in 1846 after the Treaty of Amritsar between him and the British Government, by virtue of which he obtained Kashmir, no single Government had ever held sway over them. Muslim rulers had long established their authority over Kashmir, Baltistan and Gilgit; Ladakh was independent; and Jammu, handed over in 1822 by Maharaja Ranjit Singh to Maharaja Gulab Singh, had once again passed under the hereditary rule of the Dogra Rajputs. By the end of 1840 Ladakh had been conquered by the expedition under General Zorawar Singh, first sent out by Maharaja Gulab Singh in 1834. The Dogra army met with similar success in the immediately following campaign against Baltistan. Gilgit, which had been permanently occupied by the Sikhs where they had been called in to assist against Gaur Rahman, the eldest son of the ruler of Yasin who had conquered it, went over to Maharaja Gulab Singh consequent on the Treaty of Amritsar, though it had given him only the hilly country between the Ravi and the Indus. Accounts of the intrepidity, heroism and meteoric rise of Maharaja Gulab Singh constitute one of the most thrilling chapters in the history of the nineteenth century; the task of setting them out has been ably fulfilled by K. M. Panikkar in his book, "Gulab Singh: Founder of Kashmir" (Martin Hopkinson).

The conditions in Kashmir prior to its becoming

absorbed in the territories of Dogra rulers are summed up in one broad sweep by a preoccupied official writer who disposes of it as this "much conquered" country. For the early history of Kashmir we have to go to that great work, "Rajatarangini" by Kalhana. Thanks to the edition of that work by Sir Aurel Stein and his monumental introduction to it (Constable, London) —which were enabled due to the help of the late Hon'ble Raja Suraj Kaul, C.I.E., and his son, Raja Hari Kishan Kaul, the present Prime Minister of the State,—we have an authentic and valuable record of ancient Kashmir. This historian, Kalhana's chronicle was written in 1148-49 A.D. Not until we come to the sixth century A.D., it has been stated, do we get across facts in "Rajatarangini" which can be tested. Two land-marks of earlier dates noted are that the sovereign power of Asoka extended to Kashmir, as also that of Kanishka, the Indo-Scythian ruler of Upper India. Greek and Turkish influences had apparently been felt in Kashmir by this time. From the sixth century onwards, except for the interregna of the rule of good kings like Lalitaditya and Avantivarman, chaos, internal strife and oppression prevailed till the end of Hindu rule. Feudal landlords had become powerful and between their intrigues and the tyranny of the rulers, the people were ground down. The height of misgovernment was attained during King Harsha's time, that is, during the later Hindu Rule; and

Kalhana's remarks will be construed to attribute this to Turusca (Turkish) influence. In spite of the terrible evils that had overtaken the land, it was still free from foreign conquests owing to its natural situation which offered successful resistance to the invasion of Mahmud of Ghazni in 1015 A.D. But Hindu rule was decaying.

Towards the close of the thirties of the 14th century, "Shah Mir, a powerful condottiere who had come to Kashmir from the south, deposed Queen Kota, the widow of the last Hindu Ruler, and founded a Mahomedan dynasty". Even this change did not affect the external relations or internal conditions of the country. Islam, however, had already made its way and many conversions had resulted. Sir Aurel Stein says that the conversion of the majority of the population which had been achieved by the latter half of the 14th century was gradual. He even appears to think that the tolerance of Muslim rulers at that period is illustrated by the fact that Sanskrit continued under them for a time to be the official language and the Brahmins, with their literary traditions, were still the administrators. In this context, however, two facts are noteworthy. A descendant of Chengez Khan, named Zulqadr Khan, is said, during his passing raid of Kashmir lasting eight months in the twenties of the 14th century, to have converted people forcibly to Islam; and Sikandar's name has passed down as that of one of the most fanatical of men. His rule witnessed deeds which earned for him "the characteristic epithet, *Butshikhan* or the 'Idol-breaker'" (not *Butshikhast* as Sir Aurel Stein sets it down). His successors are also stated to have carried on proselytism through force. The only reign still remembered with gratitude by the Hindus in Kashmir is that of Zain-ul-abdin (1420-70 A.D.) During this long period there was tolerance, peace and progress. Pandit Anand Koul has, however, recorded that there were only eleven Hindu families left for him to tolerate. This may be an exaggeration. Zain-ul-abdin's successors were weak or vicious; there was again an eruption of the power of territorial barons resembling the *Damaras* or feudal landholders of an earlier time whom Kalhana has brilliantly satirised or vigorously denounced.

Then came "the first direct conquest of Kashmir by a foreign invader" when Mirza Haider's inroad from Ladakh in 1532 brought the territory under his control. This event is stated to have formed part of the Moghul conquest of Kashmir. All was not yet well until Akbar ultimately incorporated Kashmir into his dominion in 1586 A.D. The Moghul rule gave Kashmir a long respite from its sufferings. Until, at all events, the time of Aurangzeb the Hindus had not much grievance. They were administrators as ever before and religious tolerance was a marked trait of the conquerors. Persecution is recorded by some to have reared its head during Aurangzeb's time ; this statement is, however, contested. That versatile scholar and writer, Sir Francis Younghusband, concludes from the absence of any remark on the misery of the people by Bernier when he visited Kashmir in 1664 A.D. that there was no oppression. But Sikh records have been found to state that, under the commands of Aurangzeb, Iftikhar Khan, who had been appointed Governor of Kashmir in 1674 A.D. " was using torture towards the Pandits in Kashmir and was forcibly converting them to Islam. He also used to seize pretty Panditani girls and make them over as gifts to the Mussalmans for their *harems*". However, it is admitted that, as the Moghul rule began to fade, tyranny was again dominant and in 1750 A.D., "the cruellest and worst rule of all," that of the Afghans, was established. Lawrence has described the period of the Afghans as one of "brutal tyranny, unrelieved by good works, chivalry or honour." Men with interest, says Younghusband in his book " Kashmir", (A and C Black, London), were appointed as governors, who wrung as much money as they could out of the wretched people of the Valley. " It was said of them," he continues, "that they thought no more of cutting off heads than of plucking a flower. One used to tie up the Hindus, two and two, in grass sacks and sink them in the Dal Lake. The poll-tax on Hindus was revived and many either fled the country, were killed or were converted to Islam." Thus, for the large part of Muslim rule, the Hindus were a hunted and persecuted people. "At last," we read, "the oppression (of the Afghans) became so unendurable that the Kashmiris turned with hope to Ranjit Singh, the powerful Sikh Ruler of the Punjab".

Under the leadership of Birbal Dar and Mirza Dar, the Hindus, anxious to end the barbarous rule of the Pathans, enlisted the support of the Lahore Government. Finally in 1819, with the help of Gulab Singh, the King of the Punjab annexed Kashmir. Under the Sikhs there was, of course, much less high-handedness and oppression; but it would seem that they were by no means humane masters. According to Moorcroft, who visited Kashmir in 1824, "everywhere the people were in the most abject condition, exorbitantly taxed by the Sikh Government, and subjected to every kind of extortion and oppression by its officers,—not one-sixteenth of the cultivable surface is in cultivation, and the inhabitants, starving at home, are driven in great numbers to the plains of Hindustan." Vigne speaks of the "light and joyous prosperity that has long fled the country on account of the shameless rapacity of the ruthless Sikhs." Moorcroft felt that "the Sikhs seemed to look upon the Kashmirians as little better than cattle ......the murder of a native by a Sikh is punished by a fine to the Government of from sixteen to twenty rupees, of which four rupees are paid to the family of the deceased if a Hindu and two rupees if a Mahomedan." Remarking on the horrors of Muslim and Sikh rule, Younghusband says, "Clearly the Kashmiris had not yet come to a haven of rest, but they were nearing it (meaning the Dogra rule)."

Into the romantic story of Maharaja Gulab Singh it is now not necessary to go. Suffice it to observe that he became the independent ruler of the areas now called the Jammu and Kashmir State, and it was, as will be evident from a perusal of "Life of Sir Henry Lawrence" by Edwardes and Merivale (Smith, Elder, and Co., London), the declared and plain intention of the British Government to maintain him in such position. Maharaja Gulab Singh, though a diplomat and a statesman as well as a great soldier, had succeeded to a terrible legacy from the previous rulers. "The State of Kashmir when Gulab Singh took it over," it is recorded, "was deplorable. The Government took from two-thirds to three-quarters of the gross produce of the land,—about three times as much as is now taken. The crops when cut by the cultivators were collected in stacks. One-half was taken as the regular Government share, and additional amounts were taken as perquisites of various kinds, leaving one-third or even only a quarter with the cultivators. Of this some was taken in kind and some in cash.

The whole system of assessment and collection was exceedingly complicated and workable only in the interests of the corrupt officials; and Government held a monopoly of the sale of grain." Pre-occupied with his new responsibilities Maharaja Gulab Singh could not do much to improve the state of affairs. Exactions were still heavy. But he ruthlessly put down crime which had swollen to fearful proportions; his tolerance and liberality in religious matters have been remarked upon by the French traveller, Vigne; as an administrator, says Frederic Drew in his book, "The Northern Barrier of India" (Edward Stanford, London), he was better than most of those of his own time; the same writer adds, "Some qualities had Gulab Singh which mitigated the effects of an administration worked on the principles above denoted (the kind of administration which Gulab Singh saw around him). He was always accessible and was patient and ready to listen to complaints"; and Gulab Singh "was not wantonly cruel."

Steady improvement, however, marked the rule of Maharaja Ranbir Singh who succeeded his father, Maharaja Gulab Singh, in 1857. He was popular and zealous for reform, but he was handicapped by not having the officials 'capable of the immense labour required to remove the terrible effects of many centuries of misgovernment." Consequently, progress was slow until towards the last years of Maharaja

Ranbir Singh's reign, but it was sure. Crimes of all kinds, it appears, became rare ; an attempt was made to assess land revenue at a fixed amount; about half a lakh of rupees was spent on education and another half a lakh on repairing the "paths" and so on. These were steps in the right direction and prove that there was a conscious and purposeful endeavour to obliterate the evil trail of the past. Maharaja Pratap Singh ascended the *gadi* in 1885. A radical transformation of the administration resulted in his time. Sir Francis Younghusband, writing nearly a quarter of a century ago, enthusiastically acknowledged the progress that was being made.

Let him speak: "First and foremost, the land revenue has been properly assessed; it has been fixed in cash for a definite number of years and the share claimed by the State has been greatly reduced. This was the great work of Sir Walter Lawrence. (Of this more in a subsequent chapter.) Then a first-rate cart-road up the Jhelum Valley has been made. A well-trained set of officials have been introduced and they have been well paid. Increased, though not yet nearly sufficient, attention has been paid to education. ....A great scheme for draining the valley, reclaiming waste land and preventing floods has been commenced. As a result and in spite of the State taking a smaller share of the cultivator's produce, the revenue has more than doubled. More land is being taken up. The population is steadily increasing. The darkest days are over, and the future is assured."

In religious matters Maharaja Pratap Singh, himself a sternly orthodox Hindu, was one of the most tolerant of men. Even to-day every section of the population loves his memory. Yet Colonel A. G. Durand, who proceeded to Gilgit in 1888, says in his book, "The Making of a Frontier" (John Murray, London), while remarking on the condition of one of his coolies, "Being a Mahomedan, he has been specially ill-used since Kashmir passed under Hindu rule." There has never been a worse travesty of facts. Maharaja Pratap Singh, then, was a good man and during his time the amelioration of the condition of the people made immense head-way. The progress has been continued and accelerated so that to-day we see a completely overhauled and beneficent system of administration. For the first time after centuries of agony, the Kashmiris under Dogra rule could realise the spirit, if they could not echo the words, of Kauthsa's hyperbolical, overpowering assurance to King Raghu :

सर्वत्र नो वार्त्तमवेहि राजन्नाथे कुतस्त्वय्यशुभं प्रजानां ।
सूर्ये तपत्यावरणाय दृष्टे : कल्पेत लोकस्य कथं तमिस्रा ॥

(Know, O, king, that we are happy everywhere. Whence will ill-being afflict your subjects ? For, how can darkness cloud a place illumined by the sun ?)

II

INCEPTION OF GOOD GOVERNMENT

WE have already seen that the work of erasing the traces of misgovernment which had lasted through centuries was begun during Maharaja Ranbir Singh's time and considerably furthered by his successor, Maharaja Pratap Singh. "Thank Heaven," gratefully gasps Pandit Anand Koul, "Kashmir was not doomed to be perpetually enveloped in darkness. A new area, brighter than ever, has happily dawned on it and it is gradually emerging from dim haze into bright light". Though a man of good works, Maharaja Pratap Singh was yet weak. It has previously been stated that, in handing over Kashmir to Maharaja Gulab Singh, the British Government had never thought of interfering with its integrity. The reasons which had moved Lord (then Sir Henry) Hardinge to part with Kashmir make a lengthy story. An official note on the Jammu and Kashmir State prepared in 1928 and K. M. Panikkar's book on Gulab Singh succinctly refute the general misconception that the

British Government had foolishly "sold" Kashmir in return for Rs. 75 lakhs. The feeling of regret at having abandoned Kashmir—which does not appear to have taken account of the political conditions then existing and the facts that the British did not even command effective possession of the territory and that, though Kashmir had been legally transferred to him in March, 1846, Maharaja Gulab Singh could get actual possession of it only in November of that year after subduing the Sikh Governor who resisted his entry—soon grew into a hope of displacing the Dogra dynasty. Thus Mrs. Hervey, in the introduction to her book, "The Adventures of a Lady in Tartary" (Hope, London), published in 1854, that is, three years before Maharaja Ranbir Singh ascended the *gadi*, says, "A knowledge, too, of Kashmir and the lands adjacent, is not without political use in times which must come with the death of the present ruler, (Maharaja Gulab Singh) whom British arms placed over it. That we shall be called in to cure the fevered, anarchical state which is sure to follow that event, is certain and the more that is known of the regions we are to possess, the more firmly we shall be enabled to hold them."

Mrs. Hervey was, in the foregoing words, revealing not merely her own expectations but those which were largely shared by others. She either did not know or did not care to remember that Maharaja

Gulab Singh had all along been friendly with the British; that, at the time when they were not faring too well in 1841 in their struggle with Afghanistan, it was Maharaja Gulab Singh's help that proved decisively valuable to them; that his neutrality when they were engaged with the Sikhs in 1846 was of the utmost benefit to them; that Kashmir had, even prior to the Treaty of 1846 with the Lahore Government, been offered to Maharaja Gulab Singh and he had rejected it; and finally that, at the time, though Kashmir had been ceded to the British by the Lahore State they had little manner of holding it. That her view was, however, neither that of Hardinge nor that of Lawrence has ample proof. In his report on the installation of Maharaja Gulab Singh, Lawrence says that he informed seven Rajahs of Iskardot and its neighbourhood, who expressed themselves satisfied with Gulab Singh, that "the Maharaja would be master within his own territory." Again, writing to Maharaja Gulab Singh on 11th April 1846, Lawrence says, "It is, therefore, strange....that you should think that in your affairs I would deviate a hair's-breadth from the terms of the Treaty." The treaty referred to is, of course, that of 1846 concluded in Amritsar, Article I of which says, "The British Government transfers and makes over for ever in independent possession to Maharaja Gulab Singh and the heirs male of his body all the hilly or mountainous country with its dependencies situated to the eastward of the River Indus and the westward of the River Ravi, including Chamba and excluding Lahul, being part of the territories ceded to the British Government by the Lahore State according to the provisions of Article IV of the Treaty of Lahore, dated 9th March, 1846." According to Article X of the Treaty, Maharaja Gulab Singh was to acknowledge the supremacy of the British Government and according to Article IX, the British Government were to give their aid to him in protecting his territories from external enemies. It will, therefore, be seen that " this treaty stands on a different footing from other treaties with Indian States. The territories of which the Maharaja was recognized as ruler were handed over to him in independent possession. While the supremacy of the British Government was acknowledged, there was no agreement on the part of the Company to guarantee the internal security of the State, Article IX merely binding the British authorities to give aid to Maharaja Gulab Singh in protecting his territories from external aggression."

It is beyond our purpose here to enter on an elaborate and detailed narrative of the first encroachments made on even the internal sovereignty of the Kashmir Durbar. The complicated history of the Gilgit frontier and the final stationing of British troops constitute an extraordinary chapter. Suffice it for the present to say that " what is known as Gilgit Agency assumed great importance .... on account of its strategic importance. Beyond the Agency on the West is Chitral and on its North meet the three Sub-Continents of Russia, India and China and the country of Afghanistan. In 1877 a British Officer was stationed as Political Agent at Gilgit. He was withdrawn in 1881, but in 1889 the Agency was re-established (under Col. A. G. Durand). The Agency consists of the Gilgit Wazarat, the Chiefship of Hunza and Nagar, the Chilas District in Indus Valley and the Governorships of Punial, Yasin and Ashkoman. The settlement of Gilgit Wazarat was completed in 1893-94." The Frontier, however, is still held in the name of the Kashmir State, in spite of the impressions that may otherwise be suggested (*vide* "The Making of a Frontier" by Col. A. G. Durand, page 243, para 2). During Maharaja Ranbir Singh's time, however, the first efforts were made to maintain a British Political Officer in Kashmir. By virtue of the exceptional treaty position of the State there had been no British Resident there. "Political relations between the State and British India were conducted through the Punjab Government upto 1877"; and a mixed court of British and Kashmir officials set up in 1872 decided civil suits between European British subjects and their servants on the one hand and the subjects of the Maharaja on the other. But in the name of looking after European visitors and eliminating the difficulties experienced by the Durbar in dealing with them for want of criminal jurisdiction, a preliminary appointment of a Political Officer who was to stay there for six months in the year, during the tourist season, was made in 1877. Gradually attempts were concerted to exalt the Political Officer into a Resident. Maharaja Ranbir Singh resisted them. The programme was, hence, temporarily given up to be successfully revived shortly after the accession of Maharaja Pratap Singh. It was an invasion of his rights, but it was accomplished due to his want of strength. The next development was the Maharaja's "voluntary abdication" in 1889. A State Council was formed to take over the administration; the Maharaja's brother, Raja Sir Amar Singh, possessed of statesmanly capacity of a high order, presided over it till 1891 when Maharaja Pratap Singh became President himself. But the Resident exercised a great deal of authority. Partial powers were restored to the Maharaja in 1905 and the Council was abolished (full powers were restored to him only in 1921); but if the immense British influence over the administration of Kashmir was due to an act of aggression, it nevertheless quickened the growth of good government. Many restrictions on the freedom of the ruler remained even after the righting of the wrong done to him. Though the present Maharaja succeeded to all the powers exercised by his grandfather, Maharaja Ranbir Singh, still it has fallen to his lot gradually to eradicate the traces left over of earlier events.

Both Maharaja Pratap Singh's own reformative spirit and the intervention of the British Government were united to speed up progress in the State. Already Sir Francis Younghusband has been noticed to have given the prime place among the reforms to the new assessment and settlement of land revenue introduced by Sir Walter Lawrence in 1887. The main features of the scheme were:—

"(*a*) The State demand was fixed for ten years.

"(*b*) As a first step towards substitution of payment in cash for payment in kind, the proportion of the latter was so fixed as to cause the least hardship to the cultivators and maintain the confidence of the city population that had long been spoon-fed by a system of State rationing.

"(*c*) The sepoys who attended at harvest to coerce the cultivators were removed.

"(*d*) *Begar* in the worst form was abolished and the cultivators who had abandoned their lands for fear of being impressed under *begar* were recalled. The *assamis* were settled in their lands.

"(*e*) Occupancy rights of Zamindars in undisputed lands were confirmed.

"(*f*) Careful enquiry was made into the status of privileged holders of land. The special rates were continued for the term of the first settlement. Lands in excess of the sanctioned area were, however, assessed at the ordinary rates even in the case of privileged holders.

"(*g*) Waste lands were entered as Khalsa, but preferential right for acquiring such land was allowed to *assamis*.

"(*h*) Permanent but non-alienable hereditary occupancy rights were vested in those who accepted the first settlement so long as the revenue was paid.

"(*i*) All land was carefully valuated on the basis of the net produce, and on the basis of previous collections, the possibility of irrigation and the number of collectors.

"(*j*) The existing revenue Agency was purified and the collection of kind was taken in hand by the Settlement Department."

"Thus," it has been remarked with justice, "those who had been taught to believe that the zamindars existed only to be exploited received a rude shock."

An agricultural department was established and the introduction of co-operative societies was encouraged. Education was modernised and made open to every one in the State. In order to meet the needs of higher education, two first grade Arts Colleges and a highly equipped Technical Institute were established. "Well equipped hospitals were established in the capitals while dispensaries in charge of qualified doctors were established in towns and most important villages.....His Highness's Government by a liberal policy of road construction opened up the State. The Jhelum Valley Road and the Banihal Cart Road together form one of the longest systems of mountain roads in the world available for wheeled traffic. Based on these principal arteries of traffic is also a net-work of small roads connecting the important towns of the State. A start was made in local self-government by the establishment of Municipalities in Jammu and Srinagar. (Now Municipalities have been established at Sopore, Baramulla, Udhampur, and Mirpur.) Systematic irrigation on modern lines was introduced in the Province of Jammu where over 1,35,450 acres are receiving water from canals constructed by the State. Big scale industries were introduced in the State, especially sericulture and the systematic exploitation of the forest wealth of the country was undertaken. The laws of the State were modernised and codified (on the lines of those obtaining in British India). Vaccination on an extensive scale was introduced in the State to prevent the outbreak of small-pox which used to take a heavy toll from the population of the Valley. To prevent outbreak of cholera, modern waterworks were established at Srinagar and Jammu." Consequent on law reform, the judiciary became independent of the executive. Oppressive taxes were abolished and the Muslim marriage tax was remitted. Certain State monopolies such as of shawl industry, were removed. Several other acts of amelioration were also undertaken. There was absolute religious neutrality on the part of the ruler who resolutely set his face against discrimination between subject and subject.

We have now the historical back-ground against which to view the progress registered during the reign of Maharaja Sir Hari Singh who succeeded Maharaja Pratap Singh. The Raj Tilak ceremonies of the new ruler were celebrated in February, 1926. During a period of less than six years he has effectively transformed the life of the people and overhauled the administration. It has been his great task to regain for his State many of its lost powers and help forward a campaign of progress which, though begun under Maharaja Ranbir Singh, was systematically pursued only during the four decades of Maharaja Pratap Singh's rule. In less than half a century in all, therefore, tremendous strides have been made. Without exaggeration, the sojourner in Kashmir to-day can find little difference between the State and any other area governed under the most modern system of administration. Unremitting efforts have been and are being made to enhance the material well-being of the people. The Maharaja does not absorb the revenues of the State to secure his comfort and further his whims,—indeed, his private property inherited from his father, Raja Sir Amar Singh, yielding an annual revenue of Rs. 24 lakhs or so has been assimilated into the State. "The annual civil list for His Highness's expenditure," says a note on the Jammu and Kashmir State prepared in 1928, "is fixed at Rs. 12* lakhs. All expenditure relating to His Highness, his staff and household is met out of this source. Grants are often made out of the privy purse for charitable purposes relating to the welfare of the subjects of the State." It is interesting as well as instructive to study the report on the administration of the State for the year 1930. The Budget grant for education in 1907 was over Rs. 2 lakhs; in 1931 the budgeted amount is almost Rs. 19½ lakhs. Primary education is free and compulsory in all municipal towns for boys† and a definite programme to assist forward higher education has been laid down. "Most of the boys affected by the regulation for compulsory attendance in Kashmir," says the report, "were Mahomedans. To make the new schools specially attrac-

*This was prior to the assimilation of His Highness's private property. The privy purse now receives 9 per cent. of the annual revenues of the State.

†For girls the scheme of compulsion has not yet been given effect to. Details are being worked out.

tive to the Mahomedans, provision was also made in the Budget for the employment of 31 Arabic teachers. The number of educational institutions for boys rose from 959 to 1,036 during the year and that of scholars from 56,009 to 63,630. The special grant for encouragement of Mahomedan scholars and scholars of the backward communities was doubled during the year. One hundred and sixty scholarships for Sikh students of the Primary, Middle, and High Schools of the State were also sanctioned. The total number of girl students rose from 6,256 in the previous year to 8,350, which means an increase over 34 per cent." The paucity of women teachers has operated as a set-back to female education, but strenuous efforts are being made to remove the handicap. The expenditure on education, we find stated in the report of 1928, "only relates to items chargeable to the account head, 'Education.' Besides this, there is, of course, other expenditure on education, such as for the construction of schools, which is charged to the Public Works Grant under the existing system of accounting and budgeting, same as is the case in British India."

In matters of medical relief and social reform immense progress has been made. The number of hospitals and dispensaries in 1926 was 60; it is now 82. Four more travelling dispensaries for special treatment of women and children have been added. A scheme was sanctioned in 1930 for the opening of five new dispensaries in each province every year till the medical needs of the people were adequately satisfied. The aim of the Government is to have one dispensary for every hundred square miles and every 30,000 of the population. Leper Asylums have been established ; funds have been provided to start centres for anti-rabic treatment at Srinagar and Jammu. It is noteworthy that the expenditure over medical relief in 1926 was less than Rs. 5½ lakhs ; the budget estimate for 1931 is just under Rs. 12 lakhs. Child welfare and maternity work have received prominent attention. Maternity blocks have been added to *zenana* hospitals ; and untrained *dais* are being severely discouraged. Juvenile smoking has been prevented. Laws against kidnapping and traffic in women have been stiffened. There are depressed classes only in Jammu and their disabilities have been removed. Child marriage has been abolished ; immature boys and girls below the ages of eighteen and fourteen respectively may not now be thrust into matrimony. A preliminary survey has been made for creating a model town at Srinagar ; arrangements have been made for drinking fountains, baths, shelters, bazars, business centres and drainage. Particular care has been devoted to the improvement of sanitation. The number of co-operative societies, according to the report for 1930, increased from 2,716 to 2,916, the working capital from Rs. 78,93,608 to 89,42,782 and the membership from 57,100 to 63,364. The Agricultural credit societies increased from 2,349 to 2,438, their working capital from Rs. 44,42,289 to 49,43,234 and the membership from 44,163 to 45,602. Consolidation of holdings which has been attempted has been successfully pursued. The period of land settlement which had been fixed at twenty years has been extended to forty. Efforts have been made to combat usury. *Begar* or forced labour has been completely abolished. Conferences have been held at all important centres and lectures delivered to them on subjects such as agriculture and veterinary service. The system of grain control established in the State has proved a beneficent set-off against price fluctuations. We shall go more fully into this question elsewhere, but it may be noticed here that the step is significant of the anxiety of the Government to help the poorer classes of the population. Grants to the Public Works Department have shown constant increase. Remarkable headway has been made with irrigation and flood protection works. The floods problem has always remained with Kashmir. In the days of Avantivarman in the 9th century, a Kashmiri engineer, Suyya, anticipated the observations of modern engineers and endeavoured to cope with the trouble. The position now is vastly improved. In regard to control of liquor traffic, famine relief, water-supply, fire protection, installation of electricity and such other things we find enormous advance registered.

Trade and industry have been helped ; the imposts on manufactures which have elicited the amazed condemnation of observers of conditions inherited by the Dogra rulers have gone. An Industrial Board was brought into being at Srinagar in 1923. There are now a match factory, a santonin factory, several carpet weaving factories factories for willow works, tannery and knitting, a tent factory, an oil factory and many silk hand-weaving factories. A modern power-loom factory for silk weaving is shortly to be established. There is a wool expert now exploring possibilities. Efforts are being made to exploit the considerable mining resources of the State. Industrial Exhibitions have been arranged and two were held in 1929 and 1930. The attempt to accelerate the general economic development of the State has been steadily kept up.

The police is properly organized. There are no illegal exactions. Life and property are safe; the Kashmir citizen to-day is a free man on whom autocracy does not weigh as a terror. His attitude is no longer one of genuflexion,—physical, mental or moral; he is not subject to extra-legal assaults. It is a fine tribute to the assiduous labours to liberate him from physical oppression and moral bondage.

The wishes of the people to guide the Government are being ascertained by an annual conference of the ministers with their representatives. Thus, even a hurried survey of the unceasing activities of the Government of Kashmir, under the watchful direction of the Maharaja, is adequate to show what immense improvement has been effected in the condition of the people within all too short a period. Without hesitation it may be stated that the character and extent of the constructive work already achieved, if an incentive to further endeavours along the same lines, should yet be a source of pride and satisfaction to the ruler.

Lest the perspective should be missed, it is well to recall the situation of contrast that has been remedied. Before the reforms " the whole country in fact was still in the grip of a grinding officialdom and the officials were the remnants of a by-gone ignorant and destructive age, when dynasties and institutions and life itself were in daily danger, when nothing was fixed and lasting, when all was liable to change and at the risk of chance, and each man had to make what he could while he could; and when, in consequence, a man of honesty and public spirit had no more chance of surviving than a baby would have in a battle." Corruption now is ruthlessly put down; the monopolies held by the State of every conceivable article are no longer there; cultivators have not to allow lands to lie waste for fear of terrorism. Government expenditure is ordered and based on a budget; and in itself the budget is inoperative without regular sanction and approval. The financial administration is absolutely sound. The independence of the judiciary has been furthered by the creation of a High Court manned with competent judges, over whose verdict the Maharaja does not exercise revisionary powers, save the prerogative of mercy. The whole trend and purpose of the administration is not simply to make it beneficent but to render impossible going back on the happy changes that have been effected. This we shall see in the next chapter.

III

UNDER MAHARAJA SIR HARI SINGH

BEFORE proceeding further to analyse the character and consequences of Maharaja Sir Hari Singh's acts, we may pause a little to trace the genealogy of the present ruling house of Jammu and Kashmir. The sanad granted to Gulab Singh when Maharaja Ranjit Singh, the King of the Punjab, personally installed him on the *gadi* of Jammu in 1822 A. D. begins thus: "On this auspicious occasion, with extreme joy and with heart-felt love, I grant to Raja Gulab Singh, in recognition of his conscientious and loyal service, the Government of the Chakla of Jammu, which from time immemorial has been in the possession of his family." This acknowledgment bears out the fact that Gulab Singh's ancestors were the hereditary rulers of Jammu. *Gulabnama*, "a remarkable historical document," written by Dewan Kirpa Ram in Persian, traces the genealogy of Maharaja Gulab Singh "up to the dim dawn of Indian history to Shri Ram Chandraji himself" Historically, however, it is known that, in the eighteenth century, Raja Ranjit Deo, the great-grandfather of Maharaja Gulab Singh, held Jammu in independent possession. Maharaja Ranjit Singh's father and grandfather are said to have fought Ranjit Deo and Brij Lal Deo, the Rajas of Jammu. Younghusband says, "He (Maharaja Gulab Singh) was what is known as a Dogra Rajput, that is, a Rajput inhabiting the Dogra country,—the hilly country stretching down to the plains of the Punjab from the snowy range bounding Kashmir on the south. His far-away ancestors were Rajputs who, for generations, had followed war-like operations. Originally settled in Oudh or in Rajputana, they eventually moved to the Punjab, and settled at Mirpur in the Dogra country. One branch migrated to Chamba, another to Kangra, and the one to which Gulab Singh belonged to Jammu, where the great-great-granduncle of Gulab Singh—Throv Deo*—was during the middle of the eighteenth century a man of importance. In 1775 the son of Throv Deo built the palace at Jammu, and about 1788 Gulab Singh was born." (The dates given in this extract are inaccurate; for instance, Dhrov Deo reigned in Jammu at the beginning of the eighteenth century and Gulab Singh was born in 1792). There is "not the least doubt that Gulab Singh was descended in the direct male line from Raja Dhrov Deo, the Rajput prince of the Surya

* Dhrov Deo.

Vansi (solar) dynasty, who ruled over Jammu in the eighteenth century." The genealogical table given below will be of interest.

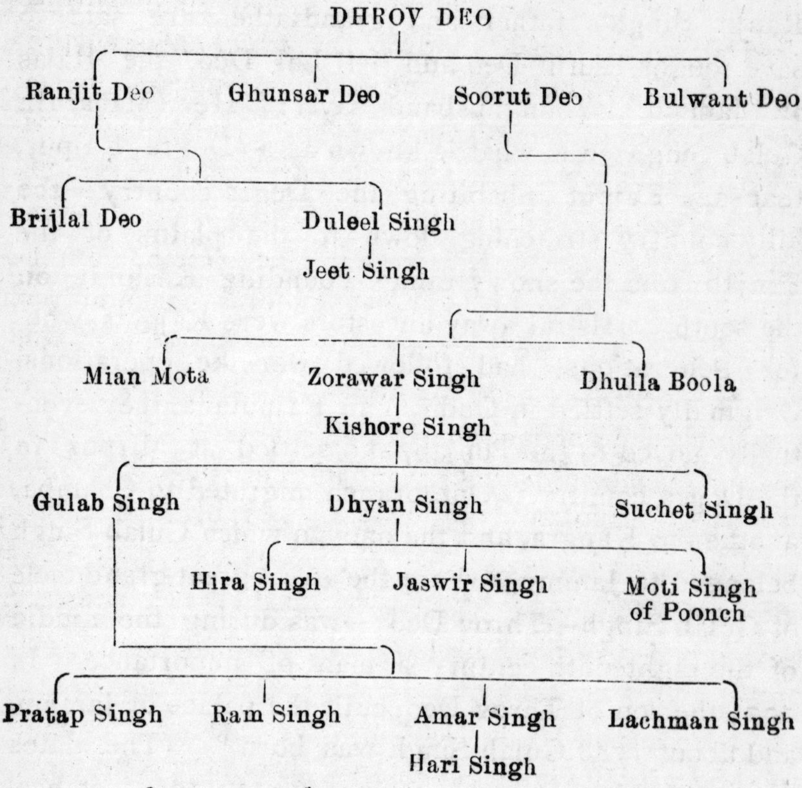

* * * *

Maharaja Ranbir Singh, the surviving son of Maharaja Gulab Singh, ascended the *gadi* of Jammu and Kashmir in 1857. On his death in 1885, Maharaja Pratap Singh succeeded him. Raja Sir Amar Singh, his (Pratap Singh's) brother, was between 1889 and 1891 the President of the State Council constituted on the "voluntary abdication" of the ruler. Thereafter, Raja Sir Amar Singh, K.C.S.I., a remarkable man and one who exercised a profound influence on the administration, was Prime Minister and Commander-in-Chief of the State forces till his death in 1907 Maharaja Pratap Singh had no son, but adopted one for spiritual purposes. Maharaja Sir Hari Singh, the present ruler of the State and the son of Raja Sir Amar Singh, ascended the *gadi* in 1926 as being the only lineal descendant alive of Maharaja Gulab Singh. As has already been seen, Maharaja Sir Hari Singh began to take part in the affairs of the State long before ascending the *gadi*. In 1915, after completing his education at Mayo College, Ajmer, he became Commander-in-Chief of the State forces at the early age of twenty. In that capacity "he took a very active part in the training and equipment of the units despatched for service overseas during the Great War and in sending reinforcements to keep them up to the regular war strength." The State forces won golden opinions wherever they served during the Great War as they had done on former occasions elsewhere. In addition to holding command of the State forces, His Highness became Senior and Foreign Member of Council in 1921. During this time he carried through an important scheme of army reorganisation. The outstanding features of the reform are thus recorded in a note issued in 1928 :—

"(1) The whole Army administration and commands have been remodelled.

"(2) The 3rd squadron of Cavalry has been raised and armed. The men for the 4th squadron are being enlisted and a full Cavalry Regiment will soon be in existence.

"(3) Mules of the best stamp have been provided for one Battery, and the Battery is fully armed and fit for service.

"(4) Two complete Infantry Units have been trained in modern mechanical weapons, half of these units being raised by recruitment. Personnel equivalent to one whole service battalion has thus been raised, trained and passed fit for service.

"(5) Two more units have been trained in the use of mechanical weapons. The battalions are complete with all technical equipment.

"(6) An innovation that His Highness has introduced into the State Army is the employment as Officers of young men of good social standing and high academic qualifications.

"(7) Another very necessary measure of reform undertaken and carried out was the construction at an estimated cost of 23 lakhs of the new Cantonment in Srinagar (opened in October 1926) which has provided the troops with excellent quarters. This Cantonment may legitimately claim to be a model of its kind by comparison with any other in India."

THE policy of rehabilitation pursued by Maharaja Pratap Singh and resolutely quickened ever since the present ruler began to have anything to do with the administration of the State soon became comprehensive in its working. In scope it embraced every direction in which betterment could be effected. Full powers had been restored to the late Maharaja Pratap Singh only four years before his death in 1925 and there was even then a residue of encroachments made on his authority. The power of the Residency continued neither in the same form nor to the same extent as before; but the State was in the unhappy position of commanding no jurisdiction over the British or British Indian subjects of the King-Emperor within its own borders which made things difficult. There were a hundred other small matters in which the limitations on the internal sovereignty of the State were being felt. The situation was unfortunate and if the Maharaja and his Government found themselves in it, both strength of purpose and delicate handling were necessary to get it modified. Gradually, little by little, the Maharaja has succeeded in re-establishing for his State its authority that, in circumstances conducive to its violation, had been abridged. The strenuous work that this process must have meant and the possibilities of the Maharaja being misunderstood and resisted can easily be imagined. It has been an uphill fight, but throughout Maharaja Sir Hari Singh has been imbued with the desire to set the position of the State right and better the lot of the people. This feeling has guided all his actions and it is necessary to grasp it in order correctly to interpret the steps that he has adopted. Owing to his unceasing endeavours, the State has regained the main part of its authority. Full criminal jurisdiction over all Indian visitors and full civil jurisdiction over all persons in the State, irrespective of their nationality, are now exercised by His Highness's courts, repairing in a large measure the anomaly of those powers being exercised by the Residency courts.

The efforts made by His Highness with a considerable degree of success to reverse the virtually mitigated internal autonomy of the State were part of a well thought out scheme. They did not constitute simply a revolt against restrictions imposed on the authority of the State obnoxious to its importance, though even so, they would have been commendable ; they were in essence an attempt at revivalism with a far-reaching purpose. One of the chief consequential acts of the new endeavour was, therefore, to carry forward the policy of manning the administration with natural born subjects of the State. But between intention and accomplishment there was a gap. We saw that Sanskrit continued to be the official language for a time under Muslim rule. Then it was changed into Persian and the Pandits who soon enough acquired proficiency in the new tongue held administrative jobs. Their aptitude in this direction stood them in good stead. Another important deviation in court language was, however, effected in the early days of Maharaja Pratap Singh's rule. When there was a switching over to Urdu, the immediate result was an influx of outsiders from the Punjab, both Hindu and Mahomedan, displacing the indigenous men. This event caused much discontent. The poise of affairs assumed a further change as English had been adopted for administrative purposes. Owing to this fact "a very large proportion of the superior appointments in the State had necessarily to be filled by imported men." The development of higher English education in the State rendered acute the "just uneasiness in the minds of His Highness's subjects." They made complaints and their validity being recognised, orders were issued from time to time that the claims of the State's subjects for appointments should be considered superior to those of outsiders. Such injunctions were, however, not adequately effective to achieve the settled purpose of the Government and bring the local people back into their own. "No appreciable result," we read, "followed from these orders owing to the vagueness of the term 'State subject.' Without a legal definition of this term it was not possible to enforce the orders of the Government with regard to the employment of outsiders." Something really useful had, therefore, to be done; in 1922, at the instance of the present ruler who was then Senior Member of Council, a Committee was appointed to define the term "hereditary State subject" and examine the entire question of naturalisation. After a thorough and exhaustive inquiry the Committee "reported that the term 'hereditary State subject' should be held to mean and include all persons born and residing within the State before the commencement of the reign of Maharaja Gulab Singhji and those who settled therein before the commencement of Samvat 1984 (1885 A.D.) and have been since permanently residing therein." In January, 1927, His Highness accepted the definition proposed by the Committee and issued an order that none who was not a "hereditary State subject" should be appointed to posts under the Government without his own express permission. *

If this policy was to succeed, it was essential that local talent should be forthcoming to be entrusted with

* It has now been recommended by the Dalal Commission, which inquired into the Kashmir disturbances of July 13, that this policy should be modified.

appointments demanding technical knowledge or special skill. "In order to secure the proper supply of trained State subjects, for the superior branches of the State services, His Highness," it may be pointed out, "has constituted a Scholarship Selection Board with a grant of Rs. 1,00,000 per annum to select scholars for special training in British India and European countries." In the first instance, the Board was instructed to get from each Minister "a statement of the vacancies likely to occur within the next three years and invite candidates for training in each department." Under the directions of His Highness a convention has now been established that the scholarships are to be divided between members of the Hindu and Muslim communities on a fifty-fifty basis. Exclusive of scholarships given by the education and other departments, the amount spent on scholarships between 1927 and March, 1931, was Rs. 3,02,918, including Rs. 60,387 reserved for Mahomedans. Among Muslim stipendiaries are two now receiving higher legal training in England; and one has completed his training in Civil Engineering in America. Special scholarships have also been awarded to Mahomedans for undergoing the LL.B. course in the Punjab. Some have also been selected for medical training, Secretariat training and training in co-operative work and accountancy. These scholarships are not awarded to Mahomedans through competition but are set apart for them so that they may not be adversely affected. His Highness issued orders last year providing Rs. 10,000 for vocational and industrial scholarships Several Hindu and Muslim youths have returned after training in Civil Engineering, Entomology, Sericulture and Medicine. The increase of 100 per cent. in expenditure on education, the award of scholarships and the constitution of a Civil Service Board to select candidates for Government appointments on the basis of an understanding that they should go in equal proportions to persons of the Hindu and Mahomedan communities are all, as has been said, the outcome of a definite and comprehensive plan. But though the scheme could take shape only gradually, His Highness had issued orders to start it even as early as 1922, that is, shortly after he became Senior and Foreign Member of Council in the days of his predecessor on the *gadi*. In pursuance of the identical policy he had also instructed that grants of lands for building and other purposes were to go only to State subjects. Non-hereditary State subjects were debarred from acquiring immovable property in the State or selling or transferring it to other than hereditary State subjects.

A Department of Civil Supplies has now been established with the specific object of assisting local enterprise. There are standing instructions that preference should be accorded to indigenous products. In regard to contracts also it has been decreed that the claims of

State subjects should have priority over those of non-subjects even if, " other things being equal, the bid of the latter is five per cent. more favourable."

A semi-State Bank is in formation. Its capital is to be Rs. 50 lakhs, half of which will be subscribed by the Government. Only State subjects can be share-holders and directors. Of the latter there is to be a non-official majority and the Chairman is to be elected. Public departments are to deposit their balances with the Bank. Government interference will be strictly confined to protecting the financial interests of the Bank and there will be a Supervisory Board to advise the directorate. In case of any emergency the claims of general depositors and creditors on assets will have priority over those of the Government.

It is now palpable that the Maharaja is not just a reformer moved by compassion to secure some slight betterment in the lot of his subjects. His motive is an intense patriotism, a burning desire to render unto Kashmiris what is theirs. He has proceeded along that one undeviating line without contenting himself with simply righting a wrong here and relieving misery there. He is the staunchest pro-Kashmiri alive and wants nothing less than making his State a happy dominion for his own subjects. Truly speaking, he is the organiser and leader of a State movement that will not bear a denial of their rights to the indigenous people. Maharaja Gulab Singh consolidated the territories now forming the State. Maharaja Sir Hari Singh is an equally great builder: he is consolidating more than territory; he is the architect of the morale of Kashmiris. It is a task more arduous than conquest to restore the self-reliance and promote the well-being of the population.

IV

ECONOMIC CONDITION OF THE PEOPLE

NOW to inquire into the economic condition of the people. The soil of Kashmir is fertile; here, more than anywhere else, Nature has been bountiful. The sufferings of the inhabitants in the past arose from tyranny and extortion rather than from an insufficiency of food resources. Famines and floods have also occasioned destitution and hunger; but the land, when cultivated, has always yielded plenty. Rice and maize are the chief crops of Kashmir, while those of Jammu are wheat and millets. The yield of rice per acre is stated to be better than in most parts of India; it would seem that forty maunds (3,280 lbs.) per acre is by no means uncommon. Of the total area of the State (84,258 square miles) the cultivable area forms 6·8 per cent. In 1921, the net cultivated area was recorded to be 4·3 per cent. of the total extent of the State and 74·5 per cent. of the cultivable area. Much progress has since been made and the process continues. But here two facts are noteworthy

Eighty per cent. of the people live by agriculture, a section of whom is made up of landless labourers. Again, while owing to the natural circumstances of the Kashmir Valley, the cultivable area is strictly limited (as will have been observed from figures cited earlier), there has been an enormous growth of population. In the seventies of the last century it is stated to have been in the neighbourhood of 6 lakhs *; now it is only somewhat below 16 lakhs. It is essential to bear these features in mind in discussing the situation of the agriculturists. So far, however, as landholding tenants are concerned, they are on the average distinctly better situated than their *confreres* in several parts of British India. Generally speaking, they are fairly well fed and well clothed though, unfortunately, as a matter of habit, they keep themselves dirty. Their housing conditions are better ; and physically they are sturdier than, say, tenants in the United Provinces who are in a deplorable position. Under the present regime the economic well-being of the agriculturists has been enhanced in a variety of ways. On the day of his accession to the *gadi*, Maharaja Sir Hari Singh made an announcement permitting landholders "to cut down trees and make use, free of charge, of all royal coniferous trees growing in areas assessed to revenue," provided that the agriculturists did not sell them. The villagers were also allowed to remove

* A lakh is a hundred thousand.

dead and fallen timber throughout the year instead of only during three months as before. His Highness gave further directions for special allotments to be made in the Budget every year for supply of drinking water in the *kandi* tract. Unpaid revenue arrears were remitted; a few months back similar relief was given costing the Treasury some lakhs. To the agriculturists other valuable forest concessions and rights in common land in the villages have also been given. The Land Alienation Act, which has been brought into force, protects the tenants from being dispossessed of their holdings by money-lenders. It may be indicated here *en passant* that the agriculturists are almost wholly Mahomedans and the money-lenders almost wholly Hindus. A further step adopted to relieve rural indebtedness is marked by the Agriculturists' Relief Regulation passed three years ago. The terms of this measure enable the agriculturist debtor to take the creditor to court for a settlement of accounts. The maximum interest which courts can award under the law is 12 per cent. per annum on condition that the entire interest allowed does not exceed 50 per cent. of the total amount decreed. The courts are also instructed to go into the accounts of a number of years and enable the judgment-debtor to liquidate his liabilities by easy payments.

We casually saw earlier that the State has established a system of grain control,—a unique experiment to guard the cultivator against the severe effects of price fluctuations. The idea will be conceded to be commendable ; and in fact, the poorer classes may anywhere in the Valley be heard to bless the Government for the measure. The acute agrarian distress discernible in the provinces of British India due to a rapid fall in prices of agricultural produce does not affect the Kashmir agriculturist who gets the same price as he did before. The Kashmir Valley food control seheme, as it is called, works this way. The cultivator is paid for his *shali* (paddy) double the cash rate at which his produce is assessed in settlement records. By giving money to the agriculturist in advance the State protects him from the necessity of borrowing either for the purpose of paying revenue or any other ; direct purchase of the agriculturist's grain by the Government eliminates the middleman and the tout. The whole of the purchased grain and what is given to the Government for that portion of revenue which is to be paid in kind, go to Srinagar where the State granary is concentrated. While it would be too much to say that its working is perfect and admits of no improvement, it is easily obvious that the scheme has helped both the cultivators and the urban classes : the former get a better price for their produce than they ever got from the middleman ; the latter get grain much cheaper than before and are protected from the cornering operations of the grain-dealers, such as were notoriously rampant in Srinagar between 1915 and 1921. For reason of the natural advantages in the State, as also of the active pursuit by the Government of an ameliorative policy, the landholding tenant in the State is, by comparison with his prototype in British India, in a truly satisfactory position. There is, however, the landless labourer who has constituted a problem. The phenomenon has not been exceptional to the Valley, but on that account the authorities have not left it alone. It was noticed earlier that the population has immensely increased while the cultivable area is limited. Consequently, these landless peasants have had in the past to migrate to British India in search of work during winter when very little work is obtainable in Kashmir. We know similar conditions exist in the submontane districts of the Punjab also. At present, however, things are more satisfactory. Flood protection and other schemes that have been undertaken provide them with plenty of work to do all the year round. If we turn to the townships, we do find people in insanitary localities and certainly even suffering. These things, however, can only go by comparison. Without the least hesitation, it may, therefore, be affirmed that there is not in Kashmir a fraction of the squalor, misery, hunger and suffering that one sees almost everywhere in British India,—not only in industrial cities. The fact that during half the year—in the cold season—a large section of the labouring classes has no fixed occupation in the Valley and has to rely on desultory engagements, living through the winter chiefly on the savings from earnings made in summer, has promoted in the Kashmir Mussalman a habit of thrift which does not exist in the same way in his brother in British India. Notwithstanding this characteristic, many of the poorer men have often to go to the money-lender, which is frightful; the saving grace of this position is that apparently usury in Kashmir is but a pale copy of that system of organised depredation prevailing in British India. That it is just usury and not the kind of day-light dacoity carried out by Pathans who forget their scriptural injunctions in the lure of money, or the more suave swindling practised by banias, Marwaris and Natukotai Chetties is small solace; but there it is, in spite of the vigorous endeavour of the Government to eliminate indebtedness.

The urban Mahomedans of Kashmir are, yet, economically generally quite well off; for, in their hands is almost completely concentrated trade, industry and skilled crafts. The many beautiful things, such as silver-ware, carpets, wicker-ware, articles of carved wood, embroidered things—silk and woollen,—papier mache creations and others too numerous to mention, for which Kashmir is famous throughou tthe world, are all produced by the Mahomedans. They are truly wonderful craftsmen and the profits that they make are enormous. But mention cannot be omitted here that the employers of skilled labour, who, by the way, are exclusively Mahomedans, treat the workmen in a scandalous manner that calls for stringency in factory laws. The wealthy among the Mussalmans are by no means negligible. But the preference of the generality of the Mussalmans for pursuits that, while requiring skill and ability, bring in satisfactory returns, has given rise to results which we may consider later. Here is certainly the chief reason why the members of the community have, as a rule, been averse to poring over musty books and educating themselves. The urban Muslims of Kashmir deriving, as they do, the benefits of their skill and training, and their rural co-religionists, those conferred by Nature on the Valley, are both economically much better placed than the Jammu Mahomedans. The Mussalmans of Jammu, who are at this disadvantage, contribute to the State army a third of its strength. But not so the Kashmir Mussalmans ; indeed, Younghusband and other writers have remarked that a Kashmiri soldier is a contradiction in terms. This, however, is by the way.

Apart from the Mahomedans the only other community of importance in the Kashmir Valley is that of the Pandits. These Brahmins numbered, according to the census of 1921 over 60,000 in all. Their proportion to the population of the State was less than 5 per cent. Now it is stated that they are about

72,000 or so. Mostly all the Pandits reside in towns and have, from time immemorial, followed occupations of a literary, priestly or administrative character. Under stress of circumstances some of them have latterly taken to other pursuits. Such men are, indeed, very few. The Kashmiri Pandits are, as an English observer has remarked, well known all over India for their acuteness, subtlety of mind, intelligence and quick-wittedness. Their contribution to arts, literature, philosophy and culture has been immense. Public life and professions in British India count many distinguished Kashmiri Pandits among their votaries. Their names constitute a dazzling array. Some of them have achieved international reputations. Any country and any age might be proud of public men like the late Pandit Motilal Nehru, Sir Tej Bahadur Sapru, and Pandit Jawaharlal Nehru; and administrators like Raja Sir Daya Kishan Kaul, and Col. Kailas Narain Haksar. In times past the Pandits of Kashmir were famous for their Sanskrit learning. People from afar used to go to them seeking knowledge and instruction. When in the dark days, particularly of Muslim rule in Kashmir, numbers of them had to migrate, they went out and established cultural contacts with places as distant as Malabar. On this subject Mr. S. Parameswara Iyer has produced an interesting note. Saivites by faith, they attracted the great leader of the rival Vaishnava school of thought,

Ramanuja, to come from Madras to Kashmir. When the State language of Kashmir was changed to Persian, the Pandits very soon acquired proficiency in that tongue and continued, in spite of troublous days, to command the esteem and admiration of foreign rulers. They were the indigenous population and as we have seen in a preceding chapter, the Kashmir Mahomedans were Pandits in origin. More than nine-tenths of the Kashmiris had been converted to Islam through force by the time the Sikhs wrested the sovereignty of Kashmir from the Pathans in the second decade of the nineteenth century. Generations of intellectual training gave the Pandits a superiority adapted to vocations for which the Mahomedans had neither prepared themselves nor cared to do so. The very intellectual qualities and capacity of the Pandit, however, rendered him fit only to be what the Mussalmans have contumeliously called *ahl-e-kalam* or "pen-pusher". The generality of Pandits consequently entered one of the learned professions or engaged themselves as clerks to traders, craftsmen and others who were mainly Mahomedans. The average Pandit, then, could not look for a competence (though undoubtedly there are among Pandits many men of wealth), but his habit of careful, almost ascetic living—a contrast to that of even the most thrifty Mussalman—has assisted him. Some Pandits have become money-lenders, but for the most part, they have had to be satisfied with modest means of livelihood. On the whole, however, their economic position is good ; they have enough for their needs because their needs are few. It cannot be too much emphasised that, like the Brahmins elsewhere, the Kashmiri Pandits as a community have only an intellectual heritage to boast of ; but, like the Brahmins of other parts, they too have provoked antagonism and jealousy, much of which is based on misunderstanding and totally false estimates. When, for instance, a homeless orphan youth begs every meal and every thread of raiment, puts up with slights and insults while seeking temporary loans of books during the hours his more fortunate contemporaries indulge in recreation, and in the end passes his examinations, is he not entitled to a job carrying a wage considerably less than that of a *bearer* or a *khansama* ? Their assiduous work and devotion to study have been of use to the Kashmiri Pandits to maintain the humble but sound economic position of the community.

In the Jammu province, the Hindus are in greater numbers. They are a few lakhs and are composed of Dogra Rajputs, Pandits and others. Economically, they are in quite a favourable position. The Dogra Rajputs are of the warrior class and they, too, like the Jammu Mahomedans, contribute a third of the strength of the State army. They may be found in the administration and other places where either valour or the advantages derived from education are of account.

The Mahomedans of Jammu, more in affinity with those of the Punjab than with those of Kashmir, are, we have noticed, much less favourably situated than their Kashmir co-religionists. They are handicapped for want of skill in the directions in which the Kashmir Mahomedans excel. Nor in agriculture do they find a haven of rest. But, like the Kashmir Mahomedans, they also have neglected education and are backward. While the Kashmiri Pandits who, according to the 1921 figures, formed 1·7 per cent. of the total population of the State of Jammu and Kashmir, constituted 80 per cent. of all those who had received or were receiving higher education, the educated among the Mahomedans were a regrettable minority. Under these conditions, the economic position of the Mussalmans of Jammu has naturally suffered.

V

COMMUNAL TROUBLES : THEIR ORIGIN

IT has been seen that Maharaja Sir Hari Singh is an intense and uncompromising pro-Kashmiri. But his feeling is not simply one of what Colonel Kailas Narain Haksar and K. M. Panikkar, in their interesting book dealing with a federal constitution for India, designate "regional particularism." It is, in fact, essentially more dynamic. His Highness is, as has been observed before, truly a revivalist. But his modernism has caused a curious position. Everything now works smoothly and well in the State. At the same time, the average man is undergoing a new experience ; he misses tha old touch between the ruler and the ruled : the lax, informal, whimsical, patriarchal contact that resulted in largesse or a kick to the plaintive suitor to favours, according as the mood of the Maharaja directed him. The present ruler is accessible to the humblest of his subjects, it is true ; but the occasions for seeking that access have now become fewer on account of the administration having been regularised. Good government* is now automatic. Life is free, but there is a lacuna. There is neither *zoolum* nor irrational patronage; yet something familiar that was there is gone. But this sense of bewilderment must be transient. The cure for the malady generated by reforms is more reforms. The most unfortunate of the State's worries, however, is the creation of influences prevailing outside the confines of the State. For a long time in British India the relations between the Hindu and Mahomedan communities have been anything but cordial. The reason partially is the educational backwardness of the Mahomedans and their economic inferiority to the Hindus and for the rest, their pathetic but unique adhesion to the idea of Islamic nationalism. The Indian Mussalman's territorial patriotism has been weakened by the conception of Muslim unity to which he still sticks unlike his brothers in faith of other countries. Even in the Punjab, where the Hindu and the Mahomedan have lived side by side and much in common between them has resulted, the latter has never succeeded in settling into the body politic. This is the more curious as, like in Kashmir, though not in the same proportion, the Mussalmans of India were originally Hindus. The leaven of foreigners among them has affected their

* In all cases where we talk of "good government" we must necessarily judge by standards of which we are aware; for, it must be remembered that there are no absolute criteria of "good government."

minds. Clever men among the administrators of the country were not slow to grasp the potentialities of this unfortunate phenomenon. It was easily perceptible that the Indian Mussalman had been unable to bring himself to regard his domicile as more than an accident. A policy of *divide et impera* was consequently initiated. It must, however, be said that the British Government in India as such never made themselves the protagonists of the scheme. Among the official and non-official British population of India also there have been and are numerous individuals who have never supported the plan of widening the rift among the Indians. But for material purposes, this distinction has availed nothing. In the early days of swelling animosity, there were men among the Mahomedans who gave the feeling of the community a constructive direction. The noblest of them was the late Sir Syed Ahmad who readily understood that, to improve the material well-being of his co-religionists, it was urgent to introduce education among them. The Aligarh University is a monument to his great endeavour. In the political sphere, Mr. Jinnah,* possessing a keen sense of realities, stepped in to weld the mutually suspicious communities in a common friendship. We shall skip over minor events. In 1916 at Lucknow finally a pact was entered into between the Hindus and the Mussalmans which

* Alas, he has changed.

aimed at protecting the interests of the latter. But the patched-up unity did not, however, last long. The ablest as well as the most dangerous of the revolters was Mr. (now Sir) Fazl-i-Husain of the Punjab who had himself signed the Lucknow Pact and sworn allegiance to it. In 1917 the British Government made a declaration that their policy in India was to promote responsible government by stages. This was what really completed the Muslim secession.

But events occurred in 1919, the reactions of which seemed to promise lasting union between the communities. There was trouble in the Punjab and martial law followed, which was one of the factors that generated the subsequent non-cooperation movement. The Mussalmans were also aggrieved about the treaty concluded with Turkey in the Great War. Mahatma Gandhi utilised their grievance to draw them into his campaign, though the Mussalmans of the Punjab stood apart and worked the Montagu-Chelmsford Reforms. The non-cooperation and the Khilafat movements virtually became one; in fact, except mainly in Northern India, the Hindus formed the majority of people interested in and carrying on the Khilafat agitation. The late Mr. Mohamed Ali—a remarkable, if exuberant personality—and his brother joined hands with the Saint of Sabarmati. Some among the Hindus doubted the character of the communal alliance that had been effected, but before the sweeping force of the non-cooperation movement, they were nowhere. It was when things were in this state that the Moplah rebellion in Malabar took place in 1921. That tragedy decided the Hindus; the present Dr. Moonje is indeed the offspring of the horrors that the Malabar fanatics had perpetrated. The link between the communities had snapped; they were once more thrown against each other. The Hindus set their faces against communal representation and separate electorates which had been introduced for the first time under the Montagu-Chelmsford Reforms enacted in 1919.* It is unnecessary to record the many manifestations of the Hindu-Muslim ill-will which culminated in quarrels and riots over petty causes and imaginary grievances. The fact was that there was hatred between them and almost anything was sufficient to bring about an outbreak of hostility. When the Hindu Mahasabha, about the end of the first term of the life of the reformed legislatures,† organised itself to moot the nationalist idea and get the disintegrating system of separate electorates abandoned, the Muslims resisted it most strongly.

The seriousness of the situation was sought to be minimised by a unity conference held at Delhi in the

* This point is often missed.

† The Mahasabha actually became a live political body only in 1925. But the opposition to separate electorates had begun vigorously to be voiced in 1923, synchronising with the close of the first term of the reformed legislatures.

latter half of 1924; but neither that convention nor repeated later attempts have been able to create an understanding between the communities. We need not follow the whole course of the communal distemper. It is enough to note that the malady has consistently grown worse rather than otherwise. The contest between the communities has been most pronounced in the Punjab, in particular, though the spirit of enmity has pervaded other areas also where the Hindus and the Mussalmans used to live in amity. The position has been further made worse during the last few months. About the end of last year Sir Muhammad Iqbal, a poet of eminence, but one of the most dangerous sponsors of Islamic hegemony, fathered in a speech at Allahabad the notion of dismembering the country. He advocated the formation of a state within state; in elaborating his theme, he gave an impetus to the idea that the good Mussalman should turn his back on India and his face towards Mecca. The Mussalmans who, strangely enough, had forgotten the treatment accorded to them in Islamic countries in the days of *hijrat* or migration, at the time of the non-cooperation movement, enthused over the lead. It represented to them an idea more attractive than even that embodied in Mr. Shaukat Ali's tilts at windmills in Palestine and Tripoli. The scheme was, of course, to transform the whole of North-western India into a Muslim state. Kashmir falls within "the line of march" and it came to be felt that it would be an excellent thing to make it part of the Muslim state envisaged to extend from Sind to Afghanistan. The particular idea of Muslimising Kashmir had for some time been vaguely present in the minds of the Mahomedans; in 1928 articles had appeared in Lahore newspapers, like the "Muslim Outlook" and "Siasat," generously proposing that Kashmir might be handed over to Afghanistan.

The repercussions, then, of the communal situation in British India, have been felt in Kashmir and matters have been complicated by issues of no concern to the State subjects. Certain internal happenings also have availed to upset the harmony prevailing among the Kashmiris since the days of Maharaja Gulab Singh. Till lately it was the proud boast of the Indian States in general that there was no communal trouble within their borders; trouble has now come as if to admonish them not to be too sure. In Kashmir before the pernicious effects of the British Indian schisms had been felt, the relations between the Hindus and the Muslims were fraternal. Disruption, however, first began in 1924. There was a strike in the silk factory at Srinagar that year and disturbances ensued. As a result of this occurrence the Kashmir Mahomedans submitted a representation to Lord Reading, the then Viceroy, in which they took a two-fold line. One was to formulate grievances; the other and objectionable one was to say that there was no hope of justice from the ruler, the late Maharaja Pratap Singh, and so his powers should be restored to the Resident. The demands made for redress of grievances were for the creation of representative institutions; the concession of a proportion in the services to the Mahomedans on the basis of population; and the conferment of proprietory rights over lands on tenants. The matter was referred back to the State Government who appointed a Commission of three members—a European, Mr. Glancy, a Mahomedan and a Hindu—to go into it. The Commission found against the demands and took particular exception to the clause in the memorial relating to an attack on the ruler. The chief outcome of the memorial was that its originators met with punishment. Mr. Said-ud-din Shawl was externed; a Muslim Tehsildar, Mr. Noor Shah Nakshbandi, was dismissed from service; and Mr. Hassan Shah Nakshbandi's *jagir** was confiscated. These men were awarded pardon by Maharaja Sir Hari Singh after his accession to the *gadi*. With the representation the Mahomedans of Jammu had not associated themselves. The reason for this was the lack of anything in common between them and the Kashmir Mahomedans. By this time, however, a movement had erupted in the Punjab in British India under the auspices of an organisation called the All-India

* State grant of land.

Kashmir Muslim Conference, composed of people who had no touch of any kind with Kashmir itself. The moving spirits behind it were Kashmiris only in the sense in which many Pandits settled in British India add to their names the distinctive appellation, " Kashmiri ". Though originally the aim of that body was supposed to be to promote education among the Muslims of Kashmir, it gratuitously took upon itself to conduct an agitation against the Kashmir Durbar,—ostensibly in the interests of the Mussalmans of the State. But until last year no Mahomedan of Jammu or Kashmir had allied himself with that organisation which yet did not prevent it from carrying on an intensive campaign. The object, of course, was to secure for the Mussalmans of British India, especially of the Punjab, the right to be taken in State service so long at least as the local Mussalmans themselves remained unqualified.

It may be inquired in what circumstances the Kashmir Muslim demands were rejected by the Commission that inquired into them. Representative institutions were at the time considered beyond practical politics; want of supply of educated Muslim youths was deemed to necessitate their restricted admission to the services; and the demand for proprietory rights was dismissed as based on misconception and also because it was understood not to accord with the wishes of the main body of the tenantry. It may here be explained that the theory of ownership of land in Kashmir is that it is the property of the Maharaja. It does not, however, make the position of the landholder precarious. Though the landholder has no right to alienate his possession, he can will it away to his relatives in accordance with his personal law. Only to this extent is there any difference between his position and that of a proprietor. But so long as he fulfils, as landholders everywhere, the obligation to pay his revenue, the land is his own and nobody has the power to evict him. It will be absolutely wrong to conclude that the land is in anything but his perpetual possession. Why the tenantry is opposed to a change is because fragmented or small holdings are notoriously an incentive to part with them and the last condition of the zamindar* would be worse than the first. The position in regard to the education of Mussalmans is now worth analysis. Apart from the same reasons as have operated elsewhere to keep the Mahomedans educationally backward, there was one peculiar to Kashmir. We have noticed elsewhere that by far the larger portion of land is vested in their hands and they have monopolised also industry, arts, and crafts. They have, hence, been little enthusiastic about education; though they constitute—according to 1921 figures—roughly 95 per cent. of the population of Kashmir and about 76 per cent. of that of Jammu

* Landlord.

and Kashmir combined, the proportion among them of literates is about a quarter or so of that of the Kashmiri Pandits who are only 1·7 per cent. of the population of Jammu and Kashmir but form 80 per cent. of all those who have received or are receiving higher education. Indeed, as has been stated, "pen-pushing" has been to Mahomedans a matter for ridicule. Even a *hanji* or a boatman may be heard to refer to the Pandits as "those fellows that scribble". But the Hindu has been naturally inclined to education, besides which his livelihood also has lain that way.

Actually, then, the outside agitators were solely concerned with pushing forward their own interests and getting changed the policy of the Kashmir Durbar of excluding them from the administrative services in the State. The stern persistence of Maharaja Sir Hari Singh in shutting them out only irritated them the more. Vilification of the ruler and the State authorities became more and more pronounced, but it availed nothing. On the other hand, the policy of the preservation of Kashmir for Kashmiris was stiffened. The measures adopted to that end have already been recorded. The foremost among them was the institution of the Scholarship Selection Board, the original members of which were Sir Albion Banerjea, a Brahmo, Mr. Wakefield, a European, and General Janak Singh, a Hindu. The earliest selections of candidates were made on the basis of personal merit alone which was disastrous to Muslim aspirants for scholarships. Their Hindu rivals scored over them and this caused a grievance. When His Highness was informed of the situation, he promptly gave instructions that the Mussalmans should not be permitted to be frustrated by their backwardness; and that is why a convention has been in force to distribute the scholarships in equal proportion between the members of the Hindu and the Mahomedan communities. In June, 1929, however, a joint memorial was presented by the Mahomedans of Jammu and Kashmir to the Maharaja. This was the first time in their history that they had joined hands; their representation was designed to draw attention to the unfavourable position of the Mussalmans in the services as well as to certain other disabilities, such as loss of property on conversion from Hinduism to Islam. In addition, the memorial protested against the prevention of child marriage which was said to be permissible under the Mahomedan Law. At the time the ruler was pre-occupied with urgent concerns. Hence he could not receive a deputation and make a reply. The matter was, however, not allowed to rest. A Minister of State, Mr. P. K. Wattal, in whose fair-mindedness both communities had confidence, was directed to take it in hand. The constitution of the Civil Service Board was the result. This body was enjoined to adjust the communal proportions in the services through a procedure of recruitment initially laid down. One-third of the candidates were to be taken through competition; one-third through promotion; and another third through nomination. The Muslims, however, feared for themselves and considered this process to be only another elaborate way of keeping them out of the services. Their representatives were invited by the Cabinet—it was in 1930 that the Board had come into being—as the Maharaja himself was absent in England and it was explained to them that the specific policy of the Government was to adjust the communal proportions in the services, with due regard to mitigating unfairness to the men already in the employment of the State. Unhappily, there was no Mussalman either in the Cabinet or on the Civil Service Board. The nervousness thus caused was, however, dispelled by the assurance that, even in regard to lower grade appointments, instructions had gone forth that they should be awarded equally between the Hindu and Muslim candidates.

While efforts were being concerted not only to do justice to the Mahomedans but to make them feel the confidence that the Government were anxious to deal with them justly, officious meddlers from outside were becoming more and more implacable. The old saying that in Kashmir there was no middle class population signified nothing to them. Formerly there were only the feudal landlords and the lower classes. But progress of education was to usher in a class that, but for the Pandits, did not exist. To cope with it required time and a well planned programme. The Kashmir Government were doing it, but the agitator of British India who was really fighting for his hand was not to be appeased by the improving welfare of the Kashmir Mussalmans. Consequently, the All-India Kashmir Muslim Conference appointed in December, 1930, a deputation headed by the Nawab of Dacca to wait on the Maharaja of Kashmir and present to him a list of grievances. Delegates from Jammu had for the first time attended this Conference, but meanwhile the Young Men's Muslim Association of Jammu and Kashmir had devoted itself to anti-Government activities. A section of the Lahore vernacular press had intensified its personal attacks on the ruler, its slander of individual ministers and its denunciations of the administration in general ; in short, the campaign against the State had become alarmingly virulent. In February, 1931, the Cabinet met and decided to prohibit the entry into the State of the deputation led by the Nawab of Dacca. Simultaneously, the "Inqlab," a Lahore vernacular paper, was proscribed; and since it was thought that, though the members of the Young Men's Muslim Association were headstrong, they were youthful and were acting under unscrupulous leadership, they were warned of the consequences of their activities.

The most curious part of the whole affair seemed to be that some people of high position in administrative service were encouraging the anti-Government movement. Feelings were constantly being excited against the Government and in turn they also came to be directed against the Hindus who were represented as constituting the mass emblem of oppression. The prominent men among those who openly led the agitation in the State included those who had been dismissed for serious offences from the service of the State and also a deportee who, as mentioned before, had obtained his pardon and re-admission to the State through the generosity of the ruler on his accession to the *gadi* in 1926. There were others who, having nothing to do in particular, sought leadership of the Muslims through the short cut of inflaming their passions. Ignorance of the people is a life-giving nectar to the agitator. Malicious misrepresentations of the Government were spread. The dupes of the tub-thumpers being stay-at-home people and also unenlightened, did not know that the conditions of life in Muslim States were not exactly elysian; they were, therefore, easily imposed upon when imaginary advantages were described to them as inseparable from a Mahomedan government. The Kashmiri Pandit was held up as the mocking symbol of tyranny. Readily, then, the victims of demagogy came to be impressed both with their alleged tribulations and the—to them—proven iniquity of the Hindu who was stated to possess the backing of the entire administration. The uninformed Mussalmans succumbed to the moving falsehoods uttered by the so-called rescuers of the community. Though it is true that the Mussalmans—be it for reasons of their own creation—are not yet adequately represented in the services, it is wholly wrong to say that the administration has been completely Hindu. Of the five ministers, two have been Mahomedans, two Hindus and one a European. Among the High Court judges there is one, a Parsi (Sir B. J. Dalal, the Chief Justice, who was a judge of the Allahabad High Court and a man held in universal esteem), a Mahomedan and a Hindu. The personal staff of the Maharaja contains many Mahomedans. Several other high offices are filled by Mussalmans. The Maharaja has put himself out to satisfy the Muslims that he seeks their welfare. Apart from what has been done to improve the lot of the agriculturists, to promote industry and crafts which are the stronghold of the Muslims and speedily to introduce them into the administrative services, His Highness has been present at Idgah prayers to demonstrate his sympathy with his Muslim subjects; he has granted land at Jammu for Idgah and given several thousand rupees towards the same cause. Indeed, the whole trend of the policy of the ruler has led the Hindus to evince the apprehension that fair treatment would be withheld from them. Bur false propaganda overbore truth. Unluckily, also, some untoward happenings took place this year at Jammu. The agitators grasped them as if they were help sent to them by Providence. The machinery that had been set up in British India to direct action in Kashmir became galvanised. There was a constant and regular exchange of intelligence between agitators' agencies established on either side of the border of the State. Unrest was intensified and in July, notwithstanding a proclamation of good-will made by the Maharaja, it culminated in riots, arson, loot, ravaged homes, murderous assaults on men and unspeakable atrocities on women.

VI

INTERFERENCE AND ITS RESULTS

SOME at least of the men who agitated inside the State had, as has been noticed, their own scores to settle; their "friends" in British India who egged them on to keep up the unrest were actuated by divers motives. Some joined the agitation with the object of fishing in troubled waters. A typical case of such intent is provided by the request made by one of them in plain language to the Maharaja to appoint him as a minister. He had unwavering loyalty to offer in requital of the good act, but His Highness had to remain content with the loyalty that he witnessed round about him. Other men took part in the campaign against the State either because it gave them an occupation or because they would not miss an opportunity of baiting a Hindu ruler. Besides, it seemed to them that the attack on Kashmir might subserve the object of carving out a Muslim state as envisaged by Sir Muhammad Iqbal. The slogan on the lips of all these individuals variously motivated was, of course, the protection of Muslim interests that, by the way, were never in danger. It was when these relentless propagandists had made the atmosphere tense, that there occurred the incidents (alluded to in the last chapter) at Jammu which prepared the way for a serious disturbance and disastrous consequences. On 29th April of this year when the Jammu Muslims were engaged in Id prayers, Babu Khem Chand, a Sub-Inspector of Police, it appears, warned the Maulvi there against delivering a political lecture on the pretext of reading the *Khutba*. When it was pointed out to the police officer that no lecture was being delivered, he apologised for his mistake and permitted the *Khutba* to proceed. But the Maulvi declined to go on with the *Khutba* which had been interrupted. The matter was taken to the Inspector-General of Police who immediately suspended the Sub-Inspector. But the affair suited the agitators to a tee; the members of the Young Men's Muslim Association broadcast the report that the Mussalmans had been gagged from saying their *namaz* on Id day. Posters were issued to like effect. The same evening a public meeting was held at which the administration was scathingly condemned as having imperilled Islam. The Inspector-General of Police pursued his summary action against his subordinate with holding a departmental enquiry into his conduct. He invited the Mussalmans to give evidence, if they had any, against the Sub-Inspector. No Mahomedan, however, came forward to do so, on the ground that it had been intended to prosecute the Sub-Inspector. A case was then launched in the courts; the trial lasted six weeks and ultimately the accused was acquitted. On the day on which trouble occurred at Jammu, excitement ensued also at a village named Dagore in Samba Tehsil, about 15 miles from Jammu. There is a tank in the village which was being jointly used by people of both communities. But the Hindus had all along maintained that the tank was theirs. The judgment of the court had so far favoured the Hindus. On Id day the Sub-Inspector of Police in the village apprehended a breach of the peace as the Mussalmans were performing their ablutions in the tank. So he conducted an inquiry into previous practice; finding that in the past also all the Mussalmans used to perform their ablutions in the tank, he withdrew without interfering with them. His investigation was simply precautionary, but naturally it took some time to complete. This, however, provoked a complaint that the Muslims had been held up and the Id *namaz* could not be said till late in the day. A deputation from the village immediately set out for Jammu and conveyed its grievances to the Young Men's Muslim Association. This helped to feed the fury into which the Jammu Mahomedans had worked themselves on account of the local incident.

The agitation was thus vitalized; a news sheet, entitled "Kashmiri Mussalman," began to be issued from Lahore. Despite its provocative and slanderous writings, the Durbar left it alone till the middle of June whereafter they could not ignore it. The proscription of this sheet was promptly followed by the emergence of another paper under the different name of "Mazloom-i-Kashmir." It underwent the same fate as its predecessor, but it was replaced by a poster with the caption, "Maktoob-i-Kashmir," which also the authorities had to proscribe. Still assisted by the "Kashmir Mussalman," the agitators were propagating the cry, "Islam in danger," when, on June 4, an incident styled *Tauhin-i-Quran Sharif* took place further to darken the situation. Allegations were made that the Holy Quran had been dishonoured, that a Mahomedan constable had been insulted by a Hindu head constable for reading the sacred book in jail lines, and that in the resulting altercation the latter flung the Quran on the ground contemptuously telling the other not to read such trash in jail lines. Inflammatory speeches were delivered; the Government themselves were said to be supporting such insults to the Muslim religion. The cry that a formidable peril had beset Islam produced an electric effect. Fanaticism is always blind and unreasoning; and it is not the crowning sin of the members of any one community. Families have been known to have been ruined, men and women killed or injured, a deadly feud more or less permanently established even between close relatives in another part of India among the Hindus, because of a trivial, grotesque, sectarian dispute over some immaterial, so-called religious right or another. The greater the ignorance that prevails, the more, therefore, the likelihood of frenzied mass outbursts. The undiscriminating and the credulous so heard that their religion had suffered gross affronts. It was theirs to defend their faith; men had gone to heaven for smaller things than that. The susceptibilities of the unsuspecting were further played upon by unascertained and unascertainable versions of disrespect to Islam. An immediate inquiry into the jail incident was demanded. In response, His Highness deputed the Political Minister, Mr. G. E. C. Wakefield, to examine the allegations. Mr. Wakefield associated with himself two Mahomedans from Jammu selected by the leading Mussalmans of the city. The findings of this committee were that no deliberate insult had been offered to the Holy Quran by the head constable nor had it been thrown down by him, but that, during the process of rolling up the bedding of the constable, a small book, called "Panj Surah," which was on the bed, had accidentally fallen down. Mr. Wakefield reported that the Mahomedan constable had indulged in gross misrepresentation and that (1) the Mahomedan constable was to blame for mis-stating facts and causing communal unrest which might have led to a breach of the peace; and (2) that the head constable was blameworthy for losing his temper and comporting himself in a manner unbefitting one who had put in thirty years' service. While discussing the report His Highness's Council sent for the two Mir-Waizes (preachers of the community) of Kashmir and consulted them. They came to the conclusion that no *Tauhin-i-Quran* or insult to the Holy Book, had occurred and what had happened was purely accidental. They also suggested that both the constable and the head constable should be accorded punishment. Consequently, the Mahomedan constable was dismissed and the head constable retired from service; which again caused protests, because it was attempted to be made out that the Mahomedan offender had been drastically dealt with while the Hindu delinquent had been let down gently. About this time another event—tragic and infamous—had taken place. A Hindu girl, aged about 9 or 10 years, had been kidnapped. Her dead body was discovered in a drain. *Post mortem* examination showed that she had been raped. The Hindus hence became deeply excited. From the hospital they wanted to take the dead body of the unfortunate child in a procession to the burning-ground. The processionists took a route which was prohibited to them. Under the orders of the Hindu City Magistrate, Pandit Sat Lal, they were dispersed with a *lathi* charge. The Hindus were extremely agitated and started accusing the police and the authorities of partiality to the Mahomedans.

* * * *

WHEN Mr. Wakefield had gone to Jammu to inquire into the *Tauhin-i-Quran* affair, the Mahomedans had told him that they had other grievances also which they wanted to submit to His Highness. Mr. Wakefield had replied that there was an appointed day every week for the Maharaja to receive petitions and there was nothing to prevent them from taking advantage of such opportunity to state their complaints to His Highness. The Jammu Mahomedans selected four representatives and sent them in the third week of June to explain their case to the Maharaja. They duly arrived at Srinagar and were reinforced with seven representatives of their local co-religionists. But for a long time after their arrival from Jammu the Muslims did not approach His Highness. During the interval the Hindus got alarmed that the Mahomedans would take the bread out of their mouths. Already, the Hindus had vaguely felt that their future was likely to suffer and for some occult reason they were confirmed in their conclusion that the reception of the Muslim deputation by His Highness would seriously and deleteriously affect them. They hence claimed that all communities must be heard together by His Highness and a communal settlement should be arrived at on that basis. Meetings and counter-meetings were held by the members of the rival communities ; the Mahomedans of Srinagar conducted a propaganda in the mosques against their Hindu fellow-citizens. Mutual relations became more strained than ever before and the first repercussions of this situation were felt in Jammu in the social boycott of each other by the members of the contending communities. The end of June had been reached and the Government, seeing that affairs were tending badly, decided that only that community would be heard which assured the Government that it had taken steps to stop agitation in its own sphere. In these circumstances, His Highness deciding to allay excitement, issued a proclamation to all his subjects on July 9, 1931. The text of the Proclamation will bear reproduction *in extenso*. It reads :

" TO MY BELOVED PEOPLE.

" From time immemorial all communities within the State have been living on terms of closest harmony and friendship with each other and I used to take the greatest pride in the fact that we were happily free from all communal strife. I am, therefore, greatly pained to see that quite recently owing to external influences a changed and regrettable attitude is observable in certain sections in the cities of Jammu and Srinagar. This is greatly to be deplored. Two unfortunate incidents which occurred recently in

Jammu city and which could not by any stretch of imagination be associated with any action or policy of my Government and for which the responsibility rested solely on the persons involved have been seized upon and widely misrepresented inside and outside the State so as to convey to those who are not in a position to know the true facts that the policy of my Government is such that Islam is in danger. It is not my intention to deal with the details of these incidents in this message as they are being dealt with separately. So far I have preferred that my Government be judged by its actions alone. But numerous representations from my loyal subjects of all sects and creeds have reached me within the last few days to the effect that such agitation even though at present it finds no response generally is calculated to promote communal strife and might even lead to breaches of the public peace in some cases. It has accordingly been deemed necessary to make this formal announcement of the policy and intention of myself and my Government in regard to such propaganda and communal relations within the State generally.

" At the beginning of my rule I announced to you, my people, that my religion is Justice. That announcement has guided all my public acts and policies and I shall always adhere to it. I have not made, and will not permit, any discrimination against any class of my people on the grounds of religion.

The humblest of my subjects has free and direct access to me and any grievances my people may have can be submitted by them personally to me. Subject to two fundamental conditions, *viz.*,

(*i*) that political activities are confined within the law of the land, and

(*ii*) that no outside intervention is sought in any shape or form,

I have no desire whatever to suppress the legitimate requests and voice of my people, whether expressed in writing or in speech. It is my intention to give effect to these views, but I am unable to do so so long as communal tension exists, for fear of aggravating it. Consequently, the first essential is that the leaders of the various communities should take immediate action to put a stop to all political activities tending to prevent the re-establishment of friendly relations between them. As soon as it is reported to me that any community has faithfully responded to my desire, I shall be prepared to receive and consider most sympathetically any representation that community may desire to submit to me.

"Every person within the State is, and shall always be, free to practise his own religion, subject to the paramount necessity of maintaining public peace and public order. I particularly wish to refer in this connection to a malicious rumour now being spread that cow killing is shortly going to be permitted.

This malicious rumour has no foundation whatever. And it has given me great pleasure to receive from Muslim subjects spontaneous condemnation of such an insinuation or any other insinuation likely to injure the religious susceptibilities of any other community. There is no question whatever of making any change in the matter.

"In regard to recruitment for the State services prior consideration is and shall always be given to the public interest and the obligation of maintaining the efficiency of the administration at the highest possible level can never be overlooked. There is also no desire to follow a blind rule of percentages for the various communities irrespective of considerations of qualification and merit. Subject to these conditions the policy governing recruitment will be such that no one class or community should gain undue predominance in any branch of the public service and that adequate representation is secured to duly qualified Hereditary State Subjects from all classes and communities of my people. Instructions to this effect have been recently issued and I shall watch closely their practical execution by my officers.

"I have dealt above in a brief manner with what I conceive to be points of major importance with regard to which some misunderstanding prevails in certain quarters. I trust such misunderstanding will be dispelled by this authoritative enunciation of my beliefs and intentions with regard to these points. It is my aim to carry on the administration in consonance with these views in your best interests. Whenever I have found that any of you have been led into wrong action, I have always tried to make you see the error of your ways and to win you over to the right path by reasoning and conciliation. I am not a believer in false ideas of prestige, for I hold that just action is a sign of strength and not of weakness. But should, God forbid, all appeal to reason fail, I must discharge in effective manner the supreme responsibility which rests on me for the maintenance of law and order. I cannot allow my Government to be coerced by threat into unjust action and it is my duty to protect the law-abiding sections of my people from encroachments on their lawful rights. The immediate burden of maintaining law and order necessarily falls on the Magistracy and the Police whose duty it will be to see that the law is upheld at all costs, and where the law is defied, its authority will be restored. It is the duty of the Police to act impartially and with calm judgment in such emergencies and I wish to assure them that they will be supported by myself and my Government in the due discharge of their duty and will not be sacrificed to unjust clamour or intrigue.

"In conclusion, I trust that the old policy of 'live and let live' which characterised your relations with each other in the past will be restored. It is easy to excite public feeling by misrepresentation, but it is difficult to restore harmony and friendship. Do not attribute false motives to those placed in authority over you or to one another. As regards people outside the State, whether Hindus or Mahomedans, I ask them not to interfere in any way in matters concerning my State and my people, as I do not interfere in matters concerning British India and British Indians. The whole basis of political action is impaired if one political unit interferes in the domestic concerns of another. I do not wish to claim immunity from legitimate criticism of the acts and policies of my Government, which, I have no hesitation in saying, have always been designed to promote the moral and material progress of my people. It is my duty and my one aim in life to maintain the progressive character of my administration. But this end is defeated by unjustifiable outside intervention which has, within the last few weeks, done nothing but immense harm to the true interests of you all. I pray to god that you will receive the light of truth and wisdom and that you will live peacefully and happily with one another as before.

"(Sd.) HARI SINGH, G.C.I.E.,
K.C.V.O., A.D.C.,
Maharaja of Jammu and Kashmir."

The significance of the proclamation was once more misconstrued by the Mussalmans. They expressed the fear that the stress laid by the Maharaja on efficiency was to bar their entrance to the public service. Four days after the proclamation was read, came the news of the sudden and unprovoked attack on the Srinagar central jail, which will be described in the next chapter.

VII

THE JULY DISTURBANCES AND AFTER

LET us here follow the actual facts concerning the disturbances of 13th July, 1931, and the subsequent episodes. Among the flotsam and jetsam heaved up by the agitation against the State and the Hindus was a man called Abdul Qadeer. He was the cook of a European military officer stationed at Peshawar who was at the time on a visit to Kashmir. A facile speaker, he thrust himself into the campaign and made speeches not only of a seditious character but calculated to worsen the already embittered relations between the communities. He glibly cited the authority of the Quran for the things that he said; holding his hearers, as he did, on the leash of religion, he became a menace. This enterprising climber from the kitchen to the forum was apprehended and charged before the court with offences under Sections 124-A and 153-A of the Penal Code. The trial was before the Sessions Judge; it attracted crowds of Mussalmans to the court-house who impeded business by shouting

Abdul Qadeer Zindabad and *Alia-ho-Akbar*. The Chief Justice, therefore, ordered that the trial should take place within the precincts of the central jail in order to avert distraction and public demonstration. The agents of disruption translated this for the benefit of the Muslim populace to mean that the trial had been given up and an immediate sentence would be pronounced on the accused when the case was resumed. The hearing in jail fell on 13th July. On that day a mob stormed the jail and demanded admittance along with the Sessions Judge. When the Judge had passed the gates, the crowd also attempted to get in. The outer gates had been forced and the inner gates were attacked. At the suggestion of the Judge, two Muslim lawyers, representing the accused, harangued the visitors to go out of the jail precincts. Finding that there was no possibility of ingress, the crowd went out and started stoning officials and set fire to the police lines. The police force was then called in. All efforts to pacify the unruly mob proved futile. While there was commotion outside the jail, there was also disturbance inside; the prisoners tried to force the iron gates. About this time certain prisoners were being taken from the court to the jail. The crowd stoned the policemen and the prisoners were liberated. The prospect was by no means satisfactory. The District Magistrate, who had been summoned to the spot by the time, declared the crowd to be an "unlawful assembly" and ordered its dispersal. The order was defied and finding that the mob could neither be pacified nor dispersed, the District Magistrate directed fire to be opened.* The crowd fell off, but later it re-assembled and resumed stoning. It had to be dispersed with a *lathi* charge. Part of the crowd, however moved towards the Hariparbat fort; the cavalry had to pursue it and disperse it again. Another section of the recalcitrants proceeded towards a place called Maharajganj which is a business locality and loot over an extensive area followed. From Bohrikadal to Alikadal—a long stretch—the Hindu shops were raided. Other localities such as Safakadal, Ganjikhud, and Nawakadal too formed the centres of loot. Bazar streets were littered with property; books of accounts were burnt; the Hindu shopkeepers were molested; in short, pandemonium prevailed. The Hindu merchants lost lakhs worth of goods. Mr. Wakefield has affirmed that the articles were so strewn about the roads that his car could not pass; it is also his testimony that not a single Mahomedan complained to him about his premises having been invaded by the looters.

The most extraordinary portion of the story was that, almost simultaneously with the happenings at Srinagar, there was an uprising at a place named Vicharnag, some 5 or 6 miles away. It has been stated

* The Dalal Commission have found that the firing was justified and the measures taken were not excessive.

that untold atrocities were committed there; men owning lakhs were reduced to indigence and women were subjected to the worst possible cruelties and the most indecent assaults. A military force was despatched to the place, but by that time the havoc had been completed. Elsewhere the Hindus were the victims of ambuscade. Some lost their lives and many suffered physical injuries. Stray assaults continued till long after. At this serious juncture action was taken by the Government against six of the leading agitators on the advice of Mr. Wakefield. These men, three belonging to Jammu and three to Srinagar, were ordered to be arrested and interned in the fort. The Political Minister, Mr. Wakefield, had stated that the freedom of these men was a grave menace to peace; and that if these agitators who had come from Jammu were not incarcerated, the trouble that had arisen at Srinagar would be repeated at Jammu. Later on, certain representatives of Kashmir Mahomedans interceded and on the internees giving an undertaking not to misbehave in future they were enlarged at the end of July.

Meanwhile, some surprising things had taken place. It is reported that anonymous letters had been received by some officials to the effect that the Sangam bridge, many miles away from Srinagar would be burnt down. Amazingly enough, the warnings were ignored; in fact, it appears that the Maharaja had not received even a hint of the possible disturbances at Srinagar or the likelihood of incendiarism at the Sangam bridge. Notwithstanding the almost challenging information that had been furnished to the authorities, the Sangam bridge was actually burnt down three or four days after the terrible events at Srinagar. It was shortly after the act of vandalism at the Sangam bridge had been perpetrated that the ugliness of the situation was grasped in all its bearings. Until then, as has been remarked, the ruler had been kept in ignorance of details as to what was developing. When he came to know of the actual occurrences and potentialities at Srinagar, he, of course, promptly acted on his own without depending upon circumlocutory processes to fulfil themselves.* But it is staggering that he should have been kept out of touch with realities. When the position had unfolded itself in its darkest aspects, Raja Hari Kishan Kaul, an administrator of life-long experience in British India and elsewhere, was called in to take charge as Prime Minister and handle matters. Though by this time the repercussions had also been felt at Jammu, directly the moment he assumed charge, he began tackling the situation with energy and that tact born of knowledge. Gradually the confidence of the people was restored.

* The Dalal Commission have observed that but for the action taken by the Maharaja himself, devastation of the city would have been complete.

But a further opportunity had come to those in British India hostile to Kashmir. They would not miss it for anything. False reports were promptly manufactured ; the Kashmir Government were accused of "butchery" and "massacre". As a result of the incident outside the Srinagar central jail on 13th July, twelve had eventually died. But in the reports circulated in British India the number of deaths had swollen to vast proportions. It was said that peaceable folk assembled in prayer had been ruthlessly shot down ; the State police was delineated as drawn of homicidal maniacs. For the burden of the song, the tale of iniquities allegedly practised on the Muslim population was duly adopted. Incredibly enough, some English newspapers in British India, claiming to be reputable, joined in the denunciation of the Kashmir Government and the Hindu administrators. Honourable and fair-minded journalism was fulfilling itself by accepting falsehoods without even a show of investigation and by defaming the State Durbar. The lead of the self-same news sheets which these self-righteous journals used to stigmatise as constituting the "gutter-press," was enthusiastically approved and followed. In the annals of journalism in British India, there has been nothing so disgraceful, so stultifying, so utterly bereft of decency or propriety as the gleeful and unjustifiable attempt made by certain newspapers to traduce the Kashmir Administration and promote or prolong a disturbance resulting in loss of lives, destruction of property, ruin of women and murder of children. In reply to the poisonous vendetta against them the Kashmir Durbar issued on 28th July a *communiqué*, based on authoritative official reports, which is worth quoting in full. Here it is :—

"Several conflicting reports have appeared in the Press regarding the serious rioting which took place at Srinagar on July 13. Soon after the occurrence, His Highness's Government appointed a Commission of Inquiry consisting of Sir Barjor Dalal, Chief Justice as Chairman and two Judges of the High Court, one a Hindu and the other a Mahomedan, two Hindu non-officials and two Mahomedan non-officials from among leaders nominated by their community, as members to investigate the causes of the disturbances.

"His Highness's Government expecting a speedy report, was advised to defer publishing a *communique* until the Commission was in a position to make a statement of facts on the basis of the evidence presented before it. The Mahomedan non-official members, however, resigned their seats (the Hindu non-officials automatically fell out) and the Commission's work has been delayed. In the circumstances, His Highness's Government consider it necessary no longer to delay publication of such facts as have been reported by executive officers and ascertained from various sources.

"At midday on July 13 a crowd of about 5,000 people assembled outside the Jail and stormed the Jail gate with the object of rescuing a prisoner who was being tried under Sections 124-A and 153-A for sedition and for making an inflammatory speech intended to create hatred between the two communities. They rushed the outer gate and overpowered the guard. Repeated attempts were made to rush the inner gate. The Police arrested four persons, but this infuriated the mob, who started pelting the Police force with stones and brick-bats and set free four prisoners who were being escorted to the Jail. The quarters of the Jail guard were set on fire and telephone lines were cut. It was feared that all the prisoners in the Jail would escape. Attempts were made by some of the prisoners to snatch rifles from armed police, a few of whom had been seriously wounded by the mob. A *lathi* charge was made, but it proved ineffective. Therefore a warning was given to the crowd by the District Magistrate and the Deputy Inspector-General of Police—who had been summoned by telephone before the wires were cut—that fire would be opened if the unlawful assembly did not disperse, but the mob continued the onslaught.

"The Police were then ordered to fire. They fired first in the air but with no effect, and then at close range at the mob. More arrests were made thereafter. The rioters then receded and waited at a distance in two sections, one in Hariparbat and the other in a lane. Another collection of Mahomedans went in the meantime to Vicharnag, which is situated at about two miles from the Jail and about five miles from Srinagar. A third proceeded towards the city.

"The Vicharnag party perpetrated untold atrocities on the people by violence, pillage, arson and brutal assaults and indescribable outrages. They are said to have looted all they could remove and burnt and destroyed the rest. At about the same time looting started near Buherekadal. Most of the Hindu shops between Buherekadal and Safakadal including the important market of Maharajgunj, were looted and the occupants wounded.

"Some of the Punjabi shopkeepers put up a fight in defending their shops, but were overpowered by force of numbers The property lost is stated to have been worth lakhs. Hindu passers-by were assaulted and robbed, some dying from their injuries and others narrowly escaping death. *Lathis*, knives and stones formed the weapons of offence.

"Military forces were sent to the city at once and dispersed the crowd at Maharajgunj. The pillaging was stopped, but stray assaults with sticks, stones and brick-bats on Hindu passers-by continued. At places the mob assaulted the military pickets who had to fire in self-defence.

"As a result of the police firing at the Jail, six

men were killed on the spot, and some fifty were wounded. Out of the latter, four died. In two skirmishes with the military two rioters were killed and three wounded, and the latter have probably all succumbed to injuries.

"Military partrols were established and the situation taken in hand. Altogether 336 rioters were arrested. Of these 217 have been released on bail for want of sufficient evidence.

"Conditions in the city are improving, but reports are being received which go to show that agitators have been busy in the mofussil. Most of the Mahomedan shopkeepers of the city and towns outside are still observing hartal. Cases of forcible conversion of Hindus accompanied by cruelty have come to notice from the muffussil. Several speakers are reported to have created commotion by their violent speeches. Some scuffles between Hindus and Mahomedans took place on the day following the riot and complaints have been received that some Mahomedan shops were looted, although such of them as were inquired into by a high European officer turned out to be unfounded.

"The latest event is the burning of the wooden bridge over the river at Sangam which appears to be the outcome of a well-planned affair. Suitable measures are being adopted by His Highness's Government to prevent further outrages. Reliable Hindu and Muslim Officers have been deputed to make inquiries into offences committed and their work is being supervised by the higher authorities. It is hoped that peaceful conditions will be restored soon. Warning has been issued to all peaceful citizens to dissociate themselves from those who have disturbed or are disturbing the public peace."

In the meantime on 25th July, an All-India Kashmir Committee was formed at Simla and it resolved to send a deputation to Kashmir to represent grievances. Without a second thought His Highness declined to receive it. This body also resolved to make representations to the Political Department of the Government of India and the Viceroy. Failing to obtain satisfaction, it decided to approach the British Parliament. A time-limit of two months was set down to secure its objects with the Kashmir Durbar. It was also decided to observe 14th August as Kashmir Day and take out processions of Mussalmans in every city in India bearing black flags.

In parenthesis, I may mention that I met such a procession of a handful of bedraggled youths at Sialkot and inquired of them what they were doing. They were able to offer even less satisfaction than the average Mussalman in Kashmir (and even many educated men) who says that he wants his *mutalika* or demands. If questioned further, he is content innocently to refer the interrogator to his leaders.

Having told the British Indian Mussalmans to

mind their business, the Maharaja was yet prepared to listen to the complaints of his subjects. It was arranged that a deputation of Mussalmans of the State should wait on His Highness on 6th August. But the deputationists stated at the last moment that their representation had not yet been prepared. The programme was, therefore, fixed for 10th August. Again the Mussalman representatives failed to appear on the scene. For the third time an appointment was given to them for 15th August. The Mussalman spokesmen presented themselves on that day and in their memorial, a copy of which they had not, as demanded by custom, furnished to the ruler in advance, they formulated no demands but only indulged in a general tirade against the ministry. His Highness promised to give his reply in a few days; and when he gave it, he expressed the fullest confidence in his Prime Minister and disapproved of the charges preferred in the memorial as unfounded. The Muslims were again discontented. But within a few days they reached an agreement with the Government and gave a written undertaking to stop all agitation, expressing gratitude to the Prime Minister for his sympathetic handling of the situation and confessing to the fullest confidence in him. The most striking portion of their avowal was that they could settle their own affairs inside the State; indeed, they also made a frank appeal to outside Mussalmans to leave Kashmir affairs well alone.

VIII

TENDENCIES AND A WARNING

THE July disturbances were tragic: and colossally more so the sordid intrigues—of which numerous and almost incredible reports have been heard—that had caused them and the attendant loss and suffering. But so far as they signified a local affliction, the State authorities have taken suitable and effective action. To the extent to which the problem arising from the disorders was internal, we may take it that it has been solved,—at all events for the present.* The agreement reached by the Government with the malcontents is indubitably a tribute to the statesmanly capacity of the Prime Minister, though such agreements are on principle highly questionable, a point which, however, need not be developed here; the unruffled determination of His Highness not to waver from the path of justice and equal treatment to all his subjects is a proof of his magnanimity and a

*Since this was written there have been further troubles which have also been suitably handled.

vindication of his administration. During the fevered days of agitation, dangerous and treasonable slogans were sung in Kashmiri. In the grip of exploiters, the un-understanding sheepishly bleated,

Asi gachi asun shah sultan,
begonah mara gai asi mussulman,
adi ladikh kilas tai adi jail khan,
asi gachi asun panun sultan,

which, in rough paraphrase, meant,

We want none but a Muslim ruler,
Innocent folk, we Mussulmans have been killed,
Some have been interned in fort, some flung in jail,
We want none but our own ruler.

The Maharaja ignored them and re-emphasised his intention to stick to the policy that he has consistently pursued. Happily, as may have been realised, the agitation had not spread to outlying areas; it was confined chiefly to the urban spheres of Jammu and Srinagar which made it the easier to tackle it. In the end, the disorderly elements have been shown up to have been in the wrong. The Hindus who provoked themselves into protest against the settlement achieved by the authorities have been frankly told that, if their interests will not be allowed to suffer, the authorities do by no means propose that the Mussalmans should be adversely affected. No room has been left for any misapprehension ; it has been clarified that the Government are there to protect all groups and not to signify the ascendancy of any particular religious creed. Peace thus resuscitated should be long-lasting; there should, if reason prevailed, be no repetition of the horrors that dismayed the inhabitants and plunged the State in gloom. But the task of vitalising that peace remains. It cannot be done by the State alone; it demands something far more than the Maharaja's fairness to his subjects and good government in the State, both of which unquestionably exist. Here comes the part of the people and the Government of British India. They have allowed activities to go on unchecked deleterious not simply to the Kashmir State but to other States as well and to British India itself.

The true bearings of the situation must hence be grasped; the implications of the reprehensible interference of the British Indian Mussalmans do not appear to have been adequately understood. Kashmir is now an all-India affair, not because of the recent outbreak, but because that term has ceased to connote the identity of a territory and come to represent a far-reaching issue. In the first place, let us see what the meddlesomeness of the British Indian Muslims, which was really the root cause of all trouble, has done to the people of the State. It is true that the unspeakable atrocities of July were visited on the Hindus, robbing women of honour, subjecting children to assaults and reducing the wealthy to penury. In reaction, the ravage has brought creeping paralysis on the Mahomedans. Visitors have precipitately abandoned the solace and satisfaction of Kashmir this year. It must be remembered that this development means starvation to the Mussalmans, for it is they that profit by the large sums annually spent by the visitors in the Valley. House-boats have remained untenanted; the peddler is moving about with an anxious and care-worn face; the skilled workmen are unoccupied, for the cunning of their fingers cannot purchase a meal. Every year the lovely Kashmir products used to be sold to British India to the tune of a crore* and a half of rupees and the chief buyers were the Hindus. The pernicious agitation of British Indian Muslims has evoked a reprisal; it has virtually taken the form of an economic siege. Consignments of Kashmir goods worth lakhs are being promptly refused in British India. The distracted Muslim manufacturers are prepared to sell delightful and expensive articles practically for a song, but where is the market? Small wonder then that the poignant cry is heard, "Save us from our British Indian Muslim friends!" Things have been bad enough this year, and unless they are swiftly remedied, they are bound to be alarmingly so next year. But the obnoxious Muslim agitators of British India do not seem to realise the terrible injury that they are inflicting on their co-religionists in Kashmir.

The tendencies and consequences of the unwarrant-

* A crore is ten millions.

ed agitation in British India against Kashmir need also to be studied in their several other and immeasurably more menacing aspects. The case-hardened gentlemen, who have crippled their Kashmir co-religionists on the pretence of helping them, have also raised a serious question for the Government of India as well as the Indian States' governments in general. "What happens to one happens to another", said Oscar Wilde, was a thing to write on the wall for the sun to gild and the moon to silver; what has now happened to one Indian State may probably—more than probably—happen to another, or all others. The likely effects of such events on the relations between the Governments of India and the governments of the States deserve attention. Within their borders the Indian States do not allow any agitation concerning British Indian politics or against the British Indian Government. Even demonstrations of sympathy with Mahatma Gandhi have been ruthlessly put down by the States' rulers, though they themselves conceivably respect him and every one of them is professedly in favour of political advance for British India. How, then, can the British Indian Government tolerate a campaign disastrous to a State as a whole both in its conception and consequences? For the movement now directed against Kashmir there is not even the semblance of a justification; it has frankly and purely been sectarian, disruptive, and deliberately designed to overthrow the ruler. The report of the Butler Committee on the relations between the British Government and the Indian States placed its own construction on paramountcy rights, but it could not help holding that, even if the British Government could make friendly suggestions to the Princes for reforming their administrations, they could not do anything to eliminate the States' rulers. The treaty obligations of the Paramount Power impose on them the liability to protect the States; the Treaty of 1846 concluded with Kashmir makes it even more incumbent on the Government of India to discourage assaults on the internal integrity of the State. It does not mean either that all criticisms of the States' governments are to be prohibited or that States' affairs will be impervious to external influences. But any endeavour to promote treasonable activities in a State or against it is certainly to be reprobated and arrested. If the sort of attack that has gone on against Kashmir continues, the Indian States rulers are naturally bound to feel a resentment against the Government of India on account of their policy of *laissez-faire*; the Princes must experience a nervousness ill conducive to a satisfactory condition of things. No reasonable Prince or his administration is likely to take exception to constitutional representation of grievances; and Kashmir being no exception to the rule any more than any other State or any part of British India, there are conditions in it susceptible of improvement. But to strive for such a result is vastly different from promoting a disingenuous campaign which sets one section of the State's subjects against another and seeks to overthrow the ruler.

It is also to be remembered that the sort of agitation conducted against Kashmir must definitely have the effect of making the clash between the communities in British India acuter than ever. The relations between the Hindus and the Mussalmans are embittered enough already; the ugly gap between them will be widened and not closed by making a communal dead-set against any State, let alone Kashmir. The anti-Kashmir agitation has been entirely the creation of the Mussalmans of British India. Irritated, the Hindus who do not belong to Kashmir have assumed a counter-position. It may be unfortunate, but it is natural. However, natural or otherwise, the call made by men like Mr. C. Vijiaraghavachariar and Dr. Moonje to the Mussalmans to keep their hands off Kashmir—a "Hindu State"—is a warning and a threat. Without the troubles of the Indian States muddling the counsels of the communities in British India there has been a plethora of pitched battles between them. A gratuitous alignment of the guardianship of the States between the Hindus and the Muslims of British India can only make their mutual enmity deadly. Every political theory or consideration that ingenuity or unfounded fear may suggest will go to nurse the communities in hostility towards each other. Sir Muhammad Iqbal has already done his worst. While his plea for a "state within state" has upset the sense of values of some Muslims in the Indian States, it has rendered the Hindus alike of British India and the Indian States apprehensive. Coming on top of his astounding political concept for India, the Muslim campaign against Kashmir and the alliance effected between the Mussalmans of British India and their co-religionists of the State have been construed by the Hindus as a direct invitation to them to make a similar *liaison* between themselves. The results that must spring from such a division of forces are obvious. Each of the rival sections of British Indians may appear to ally itself with its respective counterpart in the States, but in its actual development this process will usher in animosities between the British Indian people and the States' people as such. If the States' rulers are provoked in the course to try and impede political progress, the plea of self-protection will be open to them. The Maharaja of Kashmir recently uttered a crisp but eloquent sentence in this behalf. The basis of political action is impaired, he pointed out, if one political unit interferes in the domestic concerns of another. It is quite true that it is possible to strain the obligations of restraint, but at the same time, it is no less true that unjustifiable intervention of the type that we have been observing is obnoxious from every point of view, whether of propriety or of expediency.

Somewhat earlier it was said that the logical outcome of the campaign against Kashmir will be a campaign against other States as well. There are two possibilities in this direction. One is that the propaganda enabled to be carried on with impunity against one State will embolden all sorts of people to make things uncomfortable for every single State on all sorts of pretexts. The delirium to which the agitation in this connection will raise public feeling will render cautious judgment impossible. Nextly, the fundamental basis of the present attack on Kashmir is that it is a Hindu State; it will be appreciated that the counteraction will take the course of an attack on the Muslim States. It is no secret that dire reprisal on Hyderabad and Bhopal has already been threatened; it has been inquired if the Hindus of Hyderabad do not constitute about 90 per cent. and those of Bhopal about 80 per cent. of the population and what their representation in the administrative services and the cabinets is. The rights and wrongs of the case will be the last thing that determines the agitation that such a challenge foreshadows. Only a few weeks ago, it was said that a Mahomedan had killed a Hindu in Bhopal and it should be accepted as a signal for a communal raid. On the face of it, the proposal was indefensible; but when passions draw forth a reply, he who pauses to argue is a fool. Further, there is no administration so perfect in this world that it can afford to resist by its own merits onslaughts on itself. Probably, the plight of the Hindu agriculturist is anything but satisfactory in Bhopal; presumably, the Hindus of Hyderabad can, when influenced, catalogue grievances that would shock the most biased friend of the State. In a word, the line of suggestion developed here means that those resolved on a quarrel will never be thwarted for lack of excuses, convincing or otherwise. It is not, therefore, claimed that a thick veil should be drawn over misgovernment and oppression. But the point is that, though a maharaja's actions may be so overboard as to strengthen him to adapt Danton's exclamation, "There are no curtains to my bed," still it will not render him or his administration safe against those determined on causing trouble for the sake of doing so. Considered almost in any of its aspects, the campaign set working against Kashmir, unless effectively and finally neutralised, is capable of creating difficulties which none can contemplate with pleasure or equanimity. The comfort or discomfort caused to the Jammu and Kashmir State occupies by itself perhaps only a minor place. It may be the sovereign test of the Government of India's adherence to their obligations to the State But the agitation is the precursor of events that will soon put everybody, who may now shrug his shoulders and proceed without notice thinking that he need not exercise his mind over the inconveniences suffered by Kashmir, "in the wrong box," as they say. There is neither principle nor provocation about the propaganda conducted against Kashmir. If there were, it should still compel the Government of India to ask of themselves what they have done in allowing free scope to personalities who will end by plunging the whole of India in confusion. If there is one thing plain as plain can be, it is that if the unprovoked, offensive, scandalous campaign against Kashmir is not scotched even at this stage, there will be internal developments in British India, perhaps unfortunate, perhaps also illogical, that will make the authorities rue their quiescence at a time when it was their peremptory and inviolable duty curtly to say to evil-doers, "Stop it."

IX

THE FUTURE

THE endeavour of this book is not to make out that everything in the garden of the life of the people of Kashmir is as lovely as world-renowned Shalimar, but to present the facts that this writer has observed and state the conclusions at which he has arrived after a searching inquiry. No special pleading is at all needful to defend the administration of the State. The Maharaja is frankly and determinedly a friend of his people; under his ægis the administration has little chance of deviating into crooked ways. The present Prime Minister, Raja Hari Kishan Kaul, is reputedly a man of remarkable talent and energy. His attitude is not vitiated by a partisan spirit. Were proof necessary, he has demonstrated that the Hindus of the State cannot take advantage of him because he happens to profess the same religion as they. The Finance Minister, Mr. P. K. Wattal, is well known as an authority on finance and economics. He is essentially a modernist; and his training as well as inclination is opposed to obscurantism or communalism. The Mussalmans confided in him until it came to be thought a duty to mistrust every Hindu. Sir Zafar Ali, a new minister, is well known in the Punjab. During the long years of service in the province he made a good name; and his later life as a judge of the High Court was blameless. An old and esteemed personality, General Janak Singh's spotless career in the State is the best witness to his straightforwardness. The Minister-in-Waiting, Col. Nawab Khusru Jung, is a Mussalman and has had varied experience. Not even the man in the moon will affirm that an administration so constituted and distinctly enjoined by His Highness scrupulously to adhere to his policy of justice, would hurt the interests of the Mussalmans or any others. The fact that the agents of destruction have not been able to formulate their demands or put their finger on misdeeds is the finest vindication of Maharaja Sir Hari Singh's rule.

It is limpid clear that the administration is wholly governed by principles of rectitude and fairness. But there is no need to pretend that there is no suffering. The stinking hovels, for example, in the city of Srinagar would contradict such an assertion. If men have been inspired to lyric transport by the grace and beauty of Kashmir, still there can be no gainsaying that grimy poverty rears its ugly head in the State. Even that admiring lover of Kashmir,

V. C. Scott O'Connor, could not omit to notice the blot on Srinagar in his pleasant book, "The Charm of Kashmir," in which otherwise he has spoken only of attractive things. But it is incontrovertible that it is nothing like the grovelling misery among the Mussalmans as well as others in British India, whose terrible silence is heard only of God. The true and definite grievance of the Kashmir Mussalmans is that they are considerably under-represented in the public services in the State.* It was of their own making; yet the fact remains that they form the overwhelming majority of the population of the State. Satisfaction to them in this regard will brook no evasion or excuse; and it is not the intention of the ruler or his ministers that injustice to the Mahomedans should be done. The steps adopted by the Maharaja for over a decade and a half now furnish the most eloquent proof of his friendliness to the Mahomedans. Indeed, as we have seen, his policy has made the Hindus nervous, for two reasons. They see a shrinking of their numbers in the services and they have few other avenues of livelihood.

Falsehood overlaid with falsehood has attempted to hold up the administration of the State as oppressive to the Mussalmans. It is a crying shame that such an intrigue should have been initiated. The

* The report of the Dalal Commission published since these words were written embodies the same conclusion.

Mahomedans of British India have, by their interference, simply sought to poison the life of the people of the State as a whole. If the subjects of the State have complaints,—where is the place in the world in which the people have none?—the authorities are willing and ready to listen to and remedy them. In the course of the insupportable agitation against the State many mendacious things and more idiotic things have been said. The All-India Kashmir Committee has held that the basis of the Muslims' trouble is the Treaty of Amritsar of 1846 concluded by the British Government with Maharaja Gulab Singh. A proper interpretation of it has been demanded. We have seen already what that Treaty guaranteed to the ruler of Jammu and Kashmir and what it has violated. In fact, if its terms are to be adhered to, the first and foremost thing that will have to be done is the withdrawal of the British Resident in the State in order to complete repairing earlier transgressions. The Mahomedan citizens of the State can find no strength to their cause in the Treaty; it must rest on the anxious concern of the ruler for their welfare, of which there are numerous proofs and their own constitutional behaviour. The busybodies of the Punjab and elsewhere have done nothing more than to destroy what Sir C. P. Ramaswami Aiyar has called that psychic, imponderable factor, good-will, among the people of the State. The future can hardly be bright if mutual annihilation inspires the Mussalmans and the Hindus. They are fellow-citizens and have ever to live together, while the malefactors from outside will be little affected by the sufferings of the people of Kashmir. The handiwork of the meddlers—by no means a proud achievement—has been one of evil. Let them do no worse.

CONCLUSION

KASHMIR is the homeland of courtesy. Despite what traducers like one Mr. Ireland, an American, who has vilified the Kashmiris in a silly book, "From Wall Street to Cashmere," may say, both the Hindus and the Mahomedans of the Valley have many beautiful traits. They are a pleasant, nice people and their proverbial hospitality has been enshrined in living verse.

While pursuing the ramifications of a painful and shocking affair, it has been my privilege to receive the kindness of individuals of all communities and in every station of life from the humblest to the highest. Darkness has latterly overshadowed their peaceful existence. One can only pray that it may be a passing cloud and that the mutual affection between the communities may, under the vivifying touch of their beneficent ruler, be restored, making the good people of Kashmir whole once again.

APPENDIX

THE TREATY OF AMRITSAR

The following is the text of the Treaty of Amritsar :—

TREATY BETWEEN THE BRITISH GOVERNMENT on the one part and MAHARAJA GULAB SINGH OF JAMMU on the other concluded on the part of the BRITISH GOVERNMENT by FREDERICK CURRIE, Esquire, and BREVET-MAJOR HENRY MONTGOMERY LAWRENCE, acting under the orders of the RIGHT HONOURABLE SIR HENRY HARDINGE, G.C.B., one of HER BRITANNIC MAJESTY'S MOST HONOURABLE PRIVY COUNCIL, GOVERNOR-GENERAL of the possessions of the EAST INDIA COMPANY, to direct and control all their affairs in the EAST INDIES and by MAHARAJA GULAB SINGH in person—1846.

ARTICLE 1

The British Government transfers and makes over for ever in independent possession to Maharaja Gulab Singh and the heirs male of his body all the hilly or mountainous country with its dependencies situated to the eastward of the River Indus and the westward of the River Ravi* including Chamba and excluding Lahul, being part of the territories ceded to the British Government by the Lahore State according to the provisions of Article IV of the Treaty of Lahore, dated 9th March, 1846.

Article 2

The eastern boundary of the tract transferred by the foregoing article to Maharaja Gulab Singh shall be laid down by the Commissioners appointed by the British Government and Maharaja Gulab Singh respectively for that purpose and shall be defined in a separate engagement after survey.

Article 3

In consideration of the transfer made to him and his heirs by the provisions of the foregoing article Maharaja Gulab Singh will pay to the British Government the sum of seventy-five Lakhs of Rupees (Nanukshahee), fifty lakhs to be paid on ratification of this Treaty and twenty-five lakhs on or before the 1st October of the current year, A.D. 1846.

Article 4

The limits of the territories of Maharaja Gulab Singh shall not be at any time changed without concurrence of the British Government.

* After the treaty, certain territorial adjustments were made with regard to Chamba and certain arrangements were made with regard to Poonj which, however, remained under the Maharaja.

ARTICLE 5

Maharaja Gulab Singh will refer to the arbitration of the British Government any disputes or questions that may arise between himself and the Government of Lahore or any other neighbouring State, and will abide by the decision of the British Government.

ARTICLE 6

Maharaja Gulab Singh engages for himself and heirs to join, with the whole of his Military Forces, the British troops, when employed within the hills or in the territories adjoining his possessions.

ARTICLE 7

Maharaja Gulab Singh engages never to take or retain in his service any British subject nor the subject of any European or American State without the consent of the British Government.

ARTICLE 8

Maharaja Gulab Singh engages to respect in regard to the territory transferred to him, the provisions of Articles V, VI and VII, of the separate Engagement between the British Government and the Lahore Durbar, dated 11th March, 1846.*

* Referring to jagirdars, arrears of revenue and the property in the forts to be transferred.

ARTICLE 9

The British Government will give its aid to Maharaja Gulab Singh in protecting his territories from external enemies.

ARTICLE 10.

Maharaja Gulab Singh acknowledges the supremacy of the British Government and will in token of such supremacy present annually to the British Government one horse, twelve shawl goats* of approved breed (six male and six female) and three pairs of Cashmere shawls.

This Treaty of ten articles has been this day settled by Frederick Currie, Esquire, and Brevet-Major Henry Montgomery Lawrence, acting under directions of The Right Honourable Sir Henry Hardinge, G.C.B., Governor-General, on the part of the British Government and by Maharaja Gulab Singh in person, and the said Treaty has been this day ratified by the seal of the Right Honourable Sir Henry Hardinge, G.C.B., Governor-General.

(Done at Amritsar the sixteenth day of March, in the year of our Lord one thousand eight hundred

* On 13th March, 1884, it was arranged by mutual consent that in future the Maharaja should present, instead of 12 goats, 10 lbs. of pashm in its natural state as brought to Kashmir from Leh, 4 lbs. of picked and assorted black wool, 4 lbs. grey wool, 4 lbs. white wool, and 1 lb. of each of the three best qualities of white yarn.

and forty-six, corresponding with the seventeenth day of Rubee-ul-Awal 1262 Jijree).

(*Signed*) H. HARDINGE (Seal)

(*Signed*) F. CURRIE.

(*Signed*) H. M. LAWRENCE.

By Order of the Right Honourable the Governor-General of India.

(*Signed*) F. CURRIE,
Secretary to the Government of India,
with the Governor-General